TOWN & COUNTRY MARKETS
· NOURISHING THE QUALITY OF LIFE ·

The town of Winslow overlooking Bainbridge Island's Eagle Harbor circa 1910. Near the turn of the century, Jitsuzo Nakata and Tom Loverich—the fathers of Town & Country Market's three founders—immigrated to Bainbridge.

Mo Nakata (left) and John Nakata, who along with Ed Loverich founded the Town & Country Market on Bainbridge Island, assist customers in the meat department during the store's grand opening on August 29, 1957.

By its fiftieth anniversary in 2007, Town & Country Markets, Inc. had expanded to six stores, including three large "destination" supermarkets branded as Central Markets.

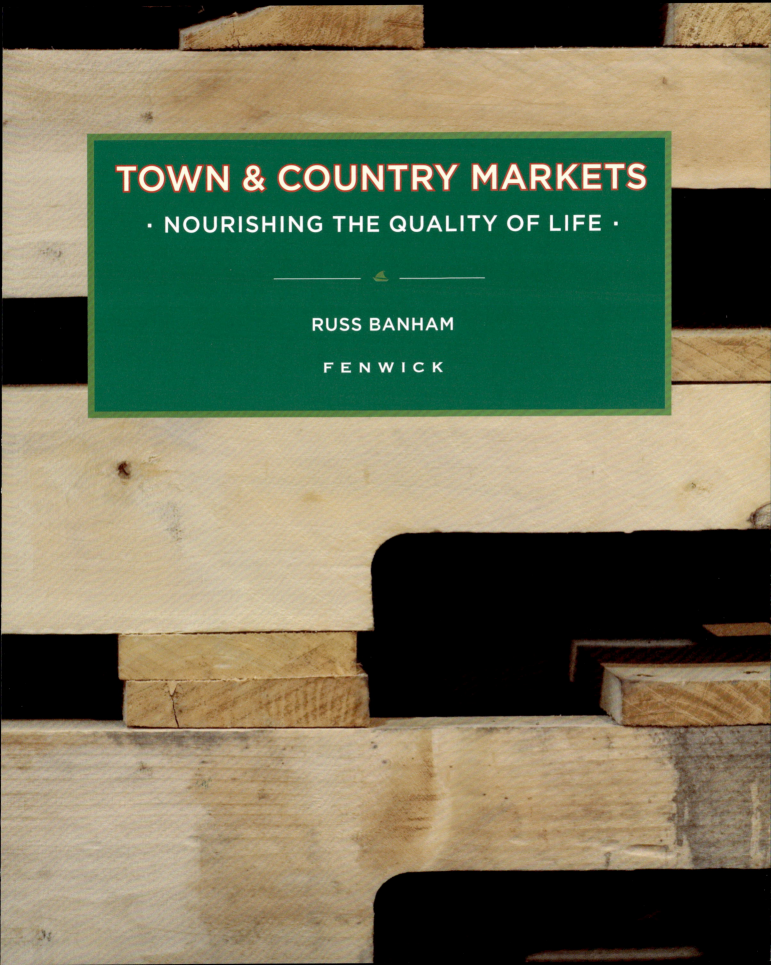

© 2007 by Town & Country Markets, Inc.

Town & Country Markets, Inc.
2208 NW Market Street #507
Seattle, Washington 98107
www.townandcountrymarkets.com

All imagery is from the collections of Town & Country Markets, Inc. and its employees, alumni, and family members, and used by permission of Town & Country Markets except for pages 6–7, 16–17, 22–23, 30–31, 38–39, 44–45, 52–53, 62–63, 68–69, 76–77, 81, 84–85, 90–91, 98–99, 102, 104–105, 111, 112–113, 115, 117, 118–119, 126, and 127, Keith Brofsky; 2–3, 18 (objects), 25, 28 (upper), 29, 43, and 54, courtesy Bainbridge Island Historical Society; 13, courtesy Bainbridge Island Historical Society, donated by Gary Loverich; 14, courtesy Bainbridge Island Historical Society, Lincoln Collection; 15, courtesy Bainbridge Island Historical Society, donated by Ray Barnecutt; 18 (upper), courtesy Bainbridge Island Historical Society, donated by Veola Lundgren; 19, courtesy Bainbridge Island Historical Society, donated by Kenneth Nakata, "In honor of our parents"; 20, courtesy Bainbridge Island Historical Society, donated by Jane Jacobson; 21, courtesy Bainbridge Island Historical Society, donated by Captain William Henshaw; 28 (object), courtesy Bainbridge Island Historical Society, donated by the Rotary Club of Bainbridge Island; 36, courtesy Bainbridge Island Historical Society, donated by the George Munro Family; 41 (upper), courtesy Bainbridge Island Historical Society, donated by Ed Loverich; 41 (lower), courtesy Bainbridge Island Historical Society, donated by the Bainbridge Island Japanese American Community; 46 (inset), courtesy Bainbridge Island Review; 47, courtesy Ralph Munro; 93 and 95, courtesy Miles Yanick & Company; and 135, Adam Smith.

All photographs of archival prints, documents, and objects were taken by Fenwick Publishing.

No part of this publication may be reproduced or transmitted in any form or by any means, electronic or mechanical, including photocopying, recording, or any information storage or retrieval system now known or to be invented, without written permission from Town & Country or its assigns.

First edition
Printed in China

16 15 14 13 12 11 10 09 08 07   1 2 3 4 5

ISBN: 0-9749510-5-6
Library of Congress Cataloging-in-Publication Data

Banham, Russ.
 Town & Country Markets : nourishing the quality of life / Russ Banham. -- 1st ed.
   p. cm.
 Includes index.
 ISBN 0-9749510-5-6
 1. Town & Country Inc. (Bainbridge Island (Wash.))--History. 2. Grocery trade--Washington (State)--Bainbridge Island--History. 3. Family-owned business enterprises--Washington (State)--Bainbridge Island--History. 4. Supermarkets--Washington (State)--Bainbridge Island--History. I. Title. II. Title: Town and Country Markets.
 HF5469.23.U64T693 2007
 381'.410979776--dc22
                            2007022817

Fenwick Publishing Group, Inc.
3147 Point White Drive, Suite 100
Bainbridge Island, Washington 98110

Fenwick Publishing produces, publishes, and markets custom publications for corporations, nonprofit organizations, and individuals.

www.fenwickpublishing.com

President and Publisher: Timothy J. Connolly
Vice President, Development: Sarah Morgans
Editorial and Production Assistant: Patrick R. Duff
Designer: Albert Treskin
Proofreader: Polly Koch
Indexer: Ken DellaPenta

CONTENTS

CHAPTER ONE
An Island Home 13

CHAPTER TWO
Launching the Flagship 35

CHAPTER THREE
Uncharted Waters 59

CHAPTER FOUR
A Destination in Sight 81

CHAPTER FIVE
New Horizons 109

FAMILY TREES 128

INDEX 130

ABOUT THE AUTHOR 135

CHAPTER ONE

An Island Home

As the crowded ship neared the Port of Tacoma, Jitsuzo Nakata marveled at the commotion. Shouting draymen and deckhands piled high a wondrous assortment of merchandise along the dock, their voices chorusing with the whistles and bells of the wharf. The air crackled with industry and progress, and Jitsuzo knew his extraordinary journey had been worth it.

The year was 1899, the turn of a century with all its attendant promise. Jitsuzo had sailed from his hometown of Agenosho, a small fishing village in the Prefecture of Yamaguchi, near Hiroshima, Japan. He was twenty-four years old, born a mere twenty-one years after Commodore Matthew C. Perry had signed the Treaty of Kanagawa with Japan on behalf of the United States. The treaty established the opportunity for trade between the two nations. A closed society since the 1600s, Japan now opened its eyes to the rest of the world. Between 1886 and 1911, an astonishing 400,000 men and women left Japan for the United States or U.S.-controlled lands like Hawaii, and significant emigration continued well into the 1920s.

What brought this earnest young fellow to the New World? He was a second son in a culture in which the oldest son inherited all parental assets. Moreover, the population in Agenosho was rising and living conditions had become impoverished. America offered opportunity. It was the fabled land of plenty, with opportunities limited only by a man's imagination, work ethic, grit, and tenacity. Jitsuzo hoped to rear and support a family, educate his children, and live in a community that supported a quality life. He simply wanted what every American's immigrant forefathers wanted—a better life.

Jitsuzo had only a sixth grade education. As a teenager, he was stationed with the Japanese army on the Taiwanese island of Formosa during the Chinese-Japanese War of 1894–95 for control of Korea, a conflict easily won by the more modern Japanese army. Korea was declared independent and China was compelled by the Treaty of Shimonoseki to cede Taiwan to Japan. After the war, Jitsuzo made the decision to leave his homeland. A friend's younger brother had moved to the Seattle area, and Jitsuzo boarded a steamer destined for the Pacific Northwest.

Upon his arrival, Jitsuzo obtained work at the Port Blakely Lumber Mill. It was the largest mill in the world, with an output of one million board feet per day at its peak. Founded in 1864 by Captain William Renton at Blakely Harbor, Bainbridge Island, the mill shaped giant western red cedars and Douglas firs as wide as a one-room schoolhouse into wood for ships, homes, and businesses. Jitsuzo loaded logs onto schooners for shipment to Hawaii, earning $1.30 a day, plus free room and board. He saved every

The irresistible lure of adventure and dreams of a better life enticed many young immigrants from Europe and Asia to trek continents and cross oceans to reach the legendary boomtowns along the American western coast. The remodeled 1940 Eagle Harbor Market on Bainbridge Island, opposite, was owned by Masaaki "John" Nakata, firstborn son of immigrants Jitsuzo and Shima Nakata. Right: A running tab for a customer named Okano at the Winslow Dock Store owned by immigrants Tom and Christina Loverich, in the days when a different kind of credit predominated.

penny he could, working long hours, day after day, alongside fellow Japanese and a smorgasbord of other immigrants—Chinese, Danish, Norwegians, Croats, Russians, Finns, and Swedes.

STAKING A CLAIM

Jitsuzo squirreled away enough money to purchase a lot on Winslow Way in the incorporated town of Winslow, the beating heart of the island. The town had formerly been called Madrone, honoring the gnarly, red-barked madrona tree that is indigenous to the area. On this site, Jitsuzo made plans to capitalize his own business—a barbershop. He had learned the trade from a Japanese friend.

The island was named for Commodore William Bainbridge, an American naval hero in the War of 1812. Five miles wide and ten miles long, Bainbridge Island is part of the San Juan archipelago in the Central Puget Sound, which connects to the Pacific Ocean via the Strait of Juan de Fuca. To the east was the booming city of Seattle, still in the thick of rebuilding following a great fire that had rendered it to ashes only a decade before. The port city now brimmed with excitement as news of a major gold strike in Canada's Yukon River Valley in 1897 reached shore. Three men had discovered gold at the junction of the Klondike River and Bonanza Creek, and over the next few years, more than 40,000 eager prospectors trooped through Seattle, purchasing supplies and securing transportation. Advertisements were placed in eastern newspapers encouraging marriageable women to try their luck west in the Emerald City.

For thousands of years, Bainbridge Island had been home to the Suquamish Indians, many of whom were still camping along the beach—fishing and collecting berries for the long winter ahead—when Jitsuzo arrived. One late spring day while scouring the beach for telltale signs of clams, Jitsuzo met a like-minded individual. His name was Thomas Loverich.

Like Jitsuzo, Tom had come to America to build a better life. He was born in 1874 on the island of Lussin, today known as Losinj, off the coast of Croatia. Southeast of Venice, the island is heralded in Greek mythology as the place where Odysseus, blown off course by stiff winds, encountered the

A labor shortage in the Puget Sound region prompted the Hall Brothers Shipyard, left, to hire hordes of able-bodied immigrants, especially men like Tom Loverich willing to settle down in the area. Loverich is seventh from the left in a white shirt and suspenders. He was a caulker at the shipyard, using tools like the ones below.

one-eyed Cyclops, Polyphemus, who feasted on much of his crew. For centuries, the island was revered as a maritime center, but its economy suffered in the late 1800s. "It was difficult to make a living by shipbuilding, fishing, or wine making," says Gary Loverich, Tom's grandson. "The political and social conditions encouraged the search for a better life somewhere else. And the New World of the Americas was open to any with the courage to make the attempt."

Tom journeyed to Vashon Island in the Puget Sound in 1897. His route from Croatia to the Puget Sound is unknown, although it is possible that he booked passage on the Transcontinental Railroad, completed in 1861. He is said to have been lured west by news of the Klondike Gold Rush and the Pacific Northwest's staggering resources, its storied rivers bursting with salmon and its abundant forests lined with giant trees. Other immigrants from the island of Lussin also trekked to the region, finding work at the Port Blakely mill or, as in Tom's case, in Vashon Island's shipyard.

RETURN TO THE HOMELAND

Both Jitsuzo and Tom did not stay long in America: each went back to his native country, albeit for a brief stay. Tom returned to Vashon Island in 1902, and the following year married seventeen-year-old Christina Cosulich, a resident of Lussin who had been born in British Columbia. The newlyweds settled on Bainbridge Island, where Tom obtained work as a caulker, or "corker," as it was pronounced, at the Hall Brothers Shipyard, which had moved that year to Bainbridge's Eagle Harbor from Port Blakely. The shipyard was renowned for its fast and beautiful schooners, many "corked" by Tom.

As for Jitsuzo, he had nearly completed building his barbershop when he was summoned in 1905 to return to Japan to fulfill his military duties in the brewing Russian-Japanese war, a conflict that grew out of the countries' imperialist ambitions. The Treaty of Portsmouth, negotiated by U.S. President Theodore Roosevelt (who received the Nobel Peace Prize for his efforts), ended the war just

7:50 AM

TOWN & COUNTRY

Longtime customer Irene Clark chats with checker Linda Papineau after completing her purchase. Irene has been shopping at T&C since 1971, and visits the store frequently to supply her Culinary Capers Catering business.

The Japanese who settled on Bainbridge Island built their own hometown of Yama, above, a word that means "mountain" in their native tongue. By the early 1900s, Yama and the neighboring Japanese-American town of Nagaya numbered more than two hundred residents, representing the largest Japanese community in the Pacific Northwest at the time. Below: Artifacts recovered from the ruins of Yama include a sake cup, eyeglasses, and a small washboard used to wash delicate women's undergarments.

before Jitsuzo arrived. With no further military obligations, Jitsuzo hoped to find a suitable woman to marry before returning to Winslow. His parents had other ideas. "Although he was not aware of it, the family matchmaker had already chosen his future mate," says Jitsuzo's grandson Wayne Nakata.

One day, Jitsuzo walked into a barbershop in Agenosho for a shave. He smiled politely at the two women who worked there. One of the women recognized Jitsuzo as the man selected to wed her coworker. "As Grandpa was put in a reclining position in the barber's chair with a hot towel covering his face, Grandma's friend pointed vigorously at Grandpa, mouthing the words, 'This is your future husband!'" says Wayne.

Jitsuzo returned to Bainbridge with his nineteen-year-old bride, Shima, in 1906. With Shima's experience cutting hair in Agenosho, the couple was determined to open up a barbershop of their own, cutting the hair of shipbuilders and mill workers. Not long after, they expanded the enterprise with a bathhouse that comprised three stalls, each with a bathtub. A sign in front of the shop read, "Haircut, Shave & Bath—50 cents."

The newlyweds lived upstairs. Next door was a meat market, and on the other side was a bakery with an upstairs dance hall called Norman's. Nearby was the Winslow Hotel. To further augment their income, the Nakatas added a laundry service. Clothes were washed by hand, washing machines having yet to be invented.

Neither Jitsuzo nor Shima spoke English, yet their social lives were full. Many Japanese families on Bainbridge, including the Kouras, Nakaos, Kitamotos, Hayashidas, and Sakais, came from the same southwestern region of Japan as they did. They lived in the hastily erected Japanese-American "towns" of Nagaya and Yama, which numbered two hundred residents by 1903. Nagaya was built in a steep ravine split by a stream south of Port Blakely that essentially cleaved Bainbridge in two and served as a water source for residents. Overlooking Nagaya from a hill on the western side of the stream was the newer town of Yama, which means "mountain" in Japanese. The two districts were unified by a wooden bridge crossing the ravine.

A DIVERSE COMMUNITY

Today, the stream and ravine are gone, having filled with soil through the years.

The newcomers lived in these towns in weathered shacks with tar-papered roofs. The homes lacked running water, so women hauled buckets from the creek to wash clothes and bathe children. Several families saved their meager earnings and ploughed them into land purchases, building farms to grow and harvest strawberries, which quickly became a mainstay of the island's economy. When the Port Blakely mill burned to the ground in 1922, much of Nagaya was torn down, and few relics of Yama exist today.

Although Bainbridge Island was home to many nationalities, the spires of their different places of worship did not divide them, and there was scant evidence of discrimination. The so-called *Issei*, or first-generation Japanese, settled comfortably in their new homeland, producing a second generation, or *Nisei*. In the middle of a fierce winter storm on January 12, 1907, in the home above their barbershop on Winslow Way, Jitsuzo and Shima welcomed their first son, named Masaaki. Their brood would include

Jitsuzo and Shima Nakata's combination laundry, barbershop, and bathhouse, above, on Bainbridge Island was frequented by shipbuilders and mill workers of many different nationalities. Jitsuzo is pictured second from right. Right: The original barbershop pole that stood outside the facility, which may have been carved by Jitsuzo.

This 1925 Winslow High School yearbook, below, features Masaaki "John" Nakata in his graduating photograph. His class was among the school's last, as it was soon succeeded by the new Bainbridge High School. Opposite: John apprenticed as a butcher at the Eagle Harbor Market owned by Charley Bremer on Winslow Way, seen here in 1910.

three more sons and six daughters, although three daughters passed away in infancy or childhood.

In the early years of their family enterprise, laundry service was provided to waterfront homes by rowboat, due to the few and rutted interior roads. In the Puget Sound, Jitsuzo dodged the Mosquito Fleet steamers that buzzed alongside carrying freight and passengers to island landings from Seattle and the Kitsap Peninsula. Some deliveries were also made by horse and buggy, but the business remained modest, and the frugal family tucked away whatever it could.

The Nakatas attended Eagle Harbor Congregational Church, the first church on the island, built in 1896 at the intersection of Winslow Way and Madison Avenue. The children went to Lincoln Elementary School across the street. Their daily chores included hauling water up to the bathhouse to fill and clean the tubs.

Jitsuzo and Shima's second son, Momoichi, born in 1920, was called "Mo." He was followed by another son, Jerry, in 1923. The sisters doted on their two younger brothers, and Jerry recalls a bit of envy when Ken was born in 1926 and stole the limelight. "My sisters turned their attention to him, and then, to make matters worse, my mother took Kenny to Japan when he was five to visit her relatives," he sighs, his eyes smiling.

Sports figured prominently among the boys, who became adept basketball and baseball players. Momoichi and his brothers Jerry and Kenny played pickup baseball against other island teams at an empty lot on Winslow Way.

In 1925, Masaaki became the first Nakata to graduate from Winslow High School. Mo and Jerry later graduated from the new Bainbridge High School built on High School Road, which was lined with cherry trees that bloomed every spring, just like in Japan. Ken would graduate from high school under far different circumstances.

Following their marriage, Tom and Christina Loverich settled into a rented house on Wing Point and, a few years later, built a small home north of the Hockett and Olsen garage on Ferncliff Avenue. Augmenting his work as a caulker, Tom fished seasonally for salmon using a purse seine, a weighted net that uses drawstrings to close it. He and Christina welcomed their first of five children, Hilda, on June 21, 1904. An extremely bright and precocious child, Hilda also was an inveterate collector; her scrapbooks provide an incisive history of the family through the years. She also tended the growing Loverich brood,

10:23 AM

GREENWOOD MARKET

Anne Herkenrath hangs updated price tags on shelves of cat food. Every week each store prints out new tags with updated pricing and sale information for hanging.

> The Loverich and Nakata families grew close through the years. Each had come from an island to an island.... Most profoundly and prophetically, their children became friends for life.

which comprised four brothers—Bill, Fred, Ed, and Francis. On occasion, she carried lunch to her father at the shipyard, an unforgettable mile's journey through the dark woods.

THE FIRST GROCERY STORE

In 1921, the Loveriches purchased the Winslow Dock Grocery Store at the foot of Madison Avenue, and moved the family upstairs. The market was situated on the dock that served as Winslow's Mosquito Fleet landing. Christina managed the store with Hilda, while Tom worked in the shipyard and pursued his fishing enterprises. Advertisements of the day announced "Winslow Dock Grocery—A Full Line of Groceries and Hardware. Orders for Stokes' Ice Cream Taken and Delivered."

During the economic boom heralded as the "Roaring Twenties," the small store's business grew with the island's rising population. Communities sprouted alongside the thirty Mosquito Fleet landings, and residents are said to have recognized their respective captains' "whistle signature" announcing arrival or departure. The Loverich children attended Lincoln Elementary School, located on Madison Avenue not far from their Winslow Dock home. Tom transported children living on the other side of Eagle Harbor to and from Winslow Dock on his boat, the *Evelyn*, so that they could attend Lincoln. "An old islander once told me he could remember hearing Tom's voice carrying across the bay," says Gary Loverich.

Tom also delivered supplies in his boat from the store to customers in Eagle Harbor or elsewhere along the beach, as did his strapping son Ed, born July 20, 1915, in the new house on Ferncliff. When the island's roads improved, some supplies were hauled in a Model T Ford, although Tom refused to drive it because its gravity-fed carburetor required traversing steep hills in reverse. Tom's sons delivered ice in the Model T to Tom's friend Jitsuzo at the barbershop, who used it to keep his meat fresh.

The Loverich and Nakata families grew close through the years. Each had come from an island to an island. Both had to learn a new language, as well as new social and political systems. Each had found economic opportunity, hired by shipyards and mills that had little antagonism toward the foreign born. And each had saved their earnings to start their own businesses. Most profoundly and prophetically, their children became friends for life.

The Nakatas struggled financially, and to augment their income, Jitsuzo bought a working strawberry farm on the corner of Wyatt Way and Weaver Avenue from the Sumiyoshi family in 1924. The purchase was made possible through the Nakatas' friendship with the Nakao family, whose son Sam, a U.S.-born citizen of legal age, signed the ownership papers for them. At the time, state and federal laws prevented immigrants from owning land in the country. Although born in the U.S., Masaaki was too young to assume legal ownership.

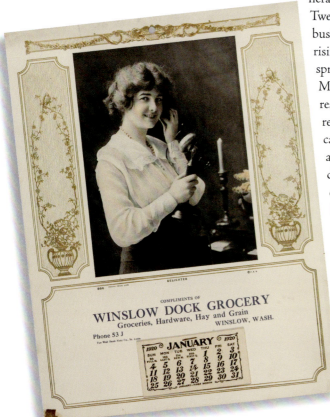

The farm had been built in 1909. It comprised a two-story farmhouse originally used to can strawberries, until local canneries came on the scene. There was no mechanical equipment, "just a single horse and plow to cultivate the fields," Jerry Nakata recalls. At planting and harvest time, many Japanese-American farmers on the island assisted each other, much like the Amish. The Nakata boys picked strawberries alongside their pal Ed Loverich, who was so physically large he had difficulty doing the task. "Ed was real lanky, and it was hard for him to stoop down and drag himself along the rows," says Kay Sakai Nakao, Mo's classmate at Bainbridge High.

NEW RESPONSIBILITIES

Masaaki ultimately took ownership of the property under the family name in 1928, when he turned twenty-one years of age. Three years later, Jitsuzo took him aside, recounts Wayne Nakata. "After reviewing the decline of the barber-laundry business and recognizing the low-yielding strawberry crop that year, Grandpa suggested to Dad, 'Maybe you ought to get a real job. How about asking Mr. Charles Bremer [the owner and operator of a local meat market] for a job?'"

Masaaki had grown up knowing Charley Bremer, proprietor of the Eagle Harbor Market. He was hired on the spot, and the shopkeeper promised to teach him the venerable butcher trade. Bremer, however, had difficulty pronouncing Masaaki's name and called him "John" or "Johnny" in his heavily accented German. It stuck and Masaaki soon made John Nakata his legal name.

On Johnny's second day of work, Bremer left the shop for awhile, leaving him to serve customers alone. In walked

Everyone in the Loverich family took part in the running of the Winslow Dock Grocery. Christina, right, helped run the day-to-day business of the store. Tom delivered goods to customers along the water by boat, while his son Bill preferred driving the island's rutted roads in the family's Model T to make deliveries, above. Alongside Bill is his sister Hilda, and in the backseat are their brothers Ed (in hat) and Francis. Opposite: A Winslow Dock Grocery calendar from 1920.

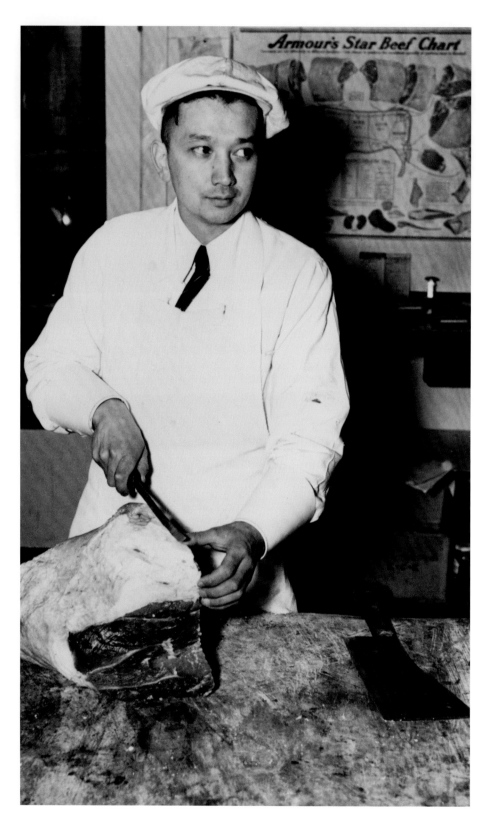

one of his former teachers, who ordered pork chops. Johnny smiled, went to the cooler, and saw two types of loins. Unfortunately, he wasn't sure which was pork and which was lamb, so he crossed his fingers, picked up a loin, and slapped it on the cutting block. "I ordered pork chops," the teacher said. To which Johnny could only reply, "Oh, I forgot." It was a baptism by fire.

His income and the part-time money earned by his brothers Mo and Jerry, who did odd jobs at the market and also learned the butcher trade, promised a steady paycheck for the family and a measure of personal security. Johnny's marriage had been arranged, and on October 1, 1933, John exchanged vows with Bainbridge resident Pauline Kawamoto in the two-story farmhouse. It was a double wedding, with John's sister Jean also marrying Pauline's brother Joe. The bridegrooms borrowed $100 to cover the costs of the wedding, reception, and honeymoon, and the happy couples shared a car to their post-wedding nest.

John Nakata, left, bought the Eagle Harbor Market in 1935 from Charley Bremer, who had taught him the butcher trade. The success of the store helped John assist his parents in paying off the mortgage on the strawberry farm they owned, an act of generosity that brought Jitsuzo to tears. Opposite: The double wedding of John and Pauline Nakata (left) and Jean Nakata and Joe Kawamoto (right).

The newlyweds moved into the farmhouse, where their first son, Don, was born on July 11, 1934. Business was brisk at the Eagle Harbor Market, and when Bremer mentioned the following year that he was interested in retiring and selling the store, John proposed buying it. Bremer accepted his offer, and John, Pauline, and Don moved into the shop's living quarters, which they remodeled.

Business continued on an upswing and was so good that John at times found himself short of meat. Jerry recalls the time a well-to-do customer briskly walked into the market and ordered a large fryer chicken. "There was only one in the barrel out back and John rummaged around in it, acting like there were several chickens in there," he says. "He then pulled up the sole chicken and said, 'Here we go. This one is really fresh and nice.' The lady looked at it and said she wanted a larger chicken. So John went back to the barrel, put the same chicken in it, and fluffed it up without her noticing. He handed it to her again and said, 'Here you go!' The woman replied, 'Perfect!—I'll take two.'"

SOMEONE TO LOOK UP TO

As the Great Depression seized the nation following the stock market crash of 1929, Tom and Christina Loverich decided the time had come to sell the Winslow Dock Store and retire. They moved their family to a house in the Hawley area of the island. Meanwhile, their six-foot, two-inch tall son Ed began thrilling islanders with his exploits as a basketball player at Bainbridge High School and, later, at the University of Washington, where he was a veritable scoring machine. Ed's nickname at UW in the mid-1930s was "Ashcan," a reference to his ability to eat as if his stomach had no bottom. After a particularly high scoring game, reporters would gush, "Ashcan cans 'em."

SHARING OUR STORIES

Mo Offers Personal Touch

Mo Nakata was a beloved man on Bainbridge Island. From his days playing basketball at Bainbridge High to his years behind the meat counter with his brother John, Mo had an effervescent personality that affected all who met him. But it was his personal touch that made customers feel special.

Tom Lamping grew up on the island in the 1950s and 1960s. When Tom was a kid, his grandfather would trek to the island on the ferry from Seattle to spend time with the grandkids and enjoy Sunday dinner with the family. Tom's grandpa passed away in 1968, and a small obituary was printed in the Seattle newspapers. "The next day it snowed heavily on the island," Tom recalls. "We were away that day, and when we arrived home that afternoon, we found a large ham at our front door. Mo Nakata had driven all the way out to Agate Point, parked at the top of our half-mile-long driveway, and walked down the steep hill, just to offer his condolences."

Tom adds that Mo's kindness was a "simple gesture, but one typical of the Nakatas, and one we haven't forgotten."

SHARING OUR STORIES

Ed Earns Bid for Olympics, Lifelong Local Fame on UW Basketball Court

It's not every day that a visit to the local supermarket yields a conversation with a bona fide basketball legend. At Town & Country, islanders old enough to remember Ed Loverich's athletic exploits in the 1930s loved few things more than chewing the fat with old "Ashcan," Ed's basketball moniker, about the day's sporting events.

Ed was a two-year University of Washington all-conference basketball player, and his UW team competed in the U.S. Olympic Trials Tournament at Madison Square Garden in 1936. A friendly, mild-mannered man, Ed was a demon on the court. The one-handed scoring virtuoso played for the UW Huskies, and one year was the league's second highest scorer. Ed is famous for inventing the one-handed push shot, which changed the history of the sport. According to a 1942 article in the *Seattle Post-Intelligencer*, Ed's coach at UW, Clarence "Hec" Edmundson, could recall "only two field goals that [Ed] scored for Washington in his varsity career that were made with both hands."

Ed always credited Edmundson, who coached twenty-seven years at UW, with inspiring him to shoot his novel way. "Coach Edmundson saw me shooting one-handed and told me to keep practicing, so I did," Ed told the *Bainbridge Island Review*. When Edmundson retired, he called Ashcan one of the best that ever played the game. The *Seattle Times* quotes Edmundson saying, "Loverich did more than any other player in the game's history to revolutionize the basketball fundamental of shooting." As for the one-handed shot, Hec often said of Ed, "He was deadly with it."

Ed's basketball days didn't end with UW. "The Filipinos wanted the Huskies to come over there," Ed told the *Review*. "Coach Edmundson got hold of eight of us kids who just finished [college]. We left Vancouver [on a twenty-one day oceangoing journey] the day after Christmas and crossed the International Date Line on New Year's, so we got two New Year's Days." One can be sure that the team, overseas for three and one-half months, celebrated both days.

Ed also was an unusual scorer, shooting baskets with one hand, as opposed to the then-customary two-handed push shot. The novel shooting method was invented by Ed, although some historians incorrectly credit Hank Luisetti from Stanford University with developing the shot. Luisetti had played against Ed and reportedly copied his style.

Jerry Nakata was in the seventh grade when Ed played for UW, and he fondly remembers when Ed and Mo took him on the ferry from the Winslow dock to a game at the university. Afterwards, a nearby Seattle malt shop customarily treated the players to free pops. "I thought life could not possibly be any better than to sit with the UW basketball team drinking malts," Jerry says.

Ed's UW Huskies team competed in the first U.S. Olympic Trials Tournament at New York City's Madison Square Garden in March 1936. Five regional teams across the country were pitted against each other. In a game against top-seeded DePaul University, Ed scored twenty points, shooting ten field goals with his one-handed shot from outside the key, leading his team to a 54-33 victory. The crowd at the Garden went wild. "Everybody thought I was a freak," Ed later told a reporter. The modern era of basketball had begun.

Mo Nakata, three years behind Ed at Bainbridge High School, sent his good pal a telegram at New York's Pennsylvania Hotel: "Come on Ashcan. Pull the lead when you play Friday. Show those punks that the Huskies from the West are hot stuff. Keep your eye on the basket and not the dames." Mo signed it with his nickname, "Porky," a reference to the meat business he had taken up.

The Huskies finished third in the tournament, just missing a chance to play at the Olympics in Berlin, officiated by Nazi leader Adolf Hitler. The Fuhrer expected his elite Aryan athletes to dominate the event. African-American sprinter Jesse Owens ruined his plans, breaking three world records and tying another in a breathtaking forty-five minutes, one of the more extraordinary milestones in track and field history.

Mo was also close friends with Ed's brother Francis. He and Mo participated in that classic rite of passage for young men—the road trip. "Francis and Mo drove down to southern California to visit Mo's sister and brother-in-law and also to catch the USC–Notre Dame game," says Gary Loverich, Francis's son and Ed's nephew. "The toll on the Golden Gate Bridge was twenty-five cents and they didn't want to pay it so they spent the night on the northern side of the bridge. They got up at four a.m., thinking they could get across the bridge before the toll keepers started work."

The country boys, surprised to learn the toll keepers worked there day and night, dug into their pockets.

Through the difficult Depression-blighted decade, John Nakata kept his nose to the grindstone. His diligence and frugality finally gave him the financial wherewithal to do something he had long aspired toward—pay off his parents' mortgage on their farm. In Japanese, there is a word—*gaman*—that describes "achievement through patience and

American sports figured prominently in the lives of the children of immigrants on Bainbridge Island. Among the Japanese-American basketball players above are Mo Nakata's brothers-in-law Kenso and Art Koura (first and fourth from left in the top row, respectively) and his brother Ken (bottom row holding the team's trophy). Right: Mo and Francis as they prepare to set out on a road trip.

11:24 AM

BALLARD MARKET

Floral department clerk Kate Robinson places a bouquet of cut roses in water. Town & Country Markets' fresh-cut flower business was launched with the one thousand bunches of cut flowers that arrived from the Aalsmeer Flower Auction in Amsterdam in 1985.

SHARING OUR STORIES

T&C Employees Help Make Occasions Special

Today, nine hundred people work at Town & Country Markets, Inc., all of them inspired to provide superior customer service. The company's employee handbook lays out this thesis plain and clear: "We must never lose touch with our customers. We talk with our customers and, most importantly, listen and hear what they're saying."

Several years ago employees listened to and heard Carolyn Goodwin's friends. She was hours away from becoming a bride, and her coworkers in Seattle wanted to send her and her groom a gift basket of champagne and chocolates. "We were to be married in our backyard on the island, and my friends couldn't find anyone in Seattle who would create and deliver a gift basket all the way to Bainbridge on short notice," Carolyn recalls. "They got the idea the day before the wedding."

Her coworkers had heard of T&C, and on a whim one of them called the store. "They were told that certainly T&C could make a basket like that," says Carolyn. "Then they asked if there was a local courier service that could get it to my house. 'No, there is no such thing over here like that,' they were told, 'but not to worry.' The kind person at T&C offered to deliver it to my house herself after work–all the way to the north end of the island. No charge. My coworkers were amazed. We received a beautifully wrapped and beribboned gift basket."

On another occasion, Esther Fox, a longtime fixture in the Bainbridge Island business community on Winslow Way, was celebrating her ninetieth birthday–a momentous occasion for her family–and her elderly brother-in-law Carl, who lived in Portland, Oregon, wanted to send her flowers but was unsure how to go about it. At the time Esther was living at the Madison Avenue Retirement Center. "He remembered a Town & Country Florist from visiting the island years ago," says Penny Lamping, Esther's granddaughter. The only problem was, there was no longer such a thing.

Nevertheless, Esther's brother-in-law called telephone information and found a phone number for T&C. He gave it a try. "Mari Loverich [the company's bookkeeper and Wayne Loverich's wife] happened to answer the phone," Penny says. "When Uncle Carl explained what he had in mind, Mari very, very kindly explained that he hadn't called the 'florist,' but that they did have a floral department, and she would be happy to take the order for the flowers [and] have the floral department put together a nice bouquet."

Mari did something else that Penny will never forget. Even though the store was not a traditional florist in the sense that it made deliveries, Mari said she would personally deliver the flowers to the retirement home. "That is what community is all about," says Penny. "Our family will always remember this kindness, along with many others from every level of employee at T&C."

perseverance." *Gaman* flowed through Jitsuzo's blood. And it flowed through John's as well.

DREAMS FULFILLED

With the mortgage paid off at the bank, John ran to the old barbershop to tell his father the good news. "Grandpa was overcome with tears of joy and jubilation," Wayne Nakata says. "He was a very emotional and visionary man. He had worked all these years, and to celebrate his son's ability to do this meant so much. The goal of his family's owning land free and clear on Bainbridge Island was fulfilled—another American Dream realized."

Business continued to flourish at Eagle Harbor Market, and John now made plans to build a new, larger store on the lot supporting the old barbershop, bathhouse, and family home. He tore the structure down in 1940, removing the tubs he had hauled water to as a boy. His entire family, including his parents, his younger siblings, and his own wife and children, now moved into the two-story farmhouse. A few weeks later, Wayne Nakata was born.

The new store hit the ground running with an ample assortment of groceries, meats, and vegetables. Sawdust was sprinkled each morning on the floor to absorb spills, scenting the air with the aroma of cut wood. Out back John had built a chicken coop for his Friday fryer special, and his brother Jerry was put in charge of raising and preparing the chickens. Mo joined John at the

In 1940 John Nakata moved the Eagle Harbor Market to the site of his parents' barbershop and laundry, tearing down the old structures to make room for the new grocery store. Jitsuzo and Shima moved to the two-story farmhouse as building commenced on the market and its clean, orderly, and inviting environs, left. The bombing of Pearl Harbor forced John to sell the store.

meat counter, while Pauline Nakata and Kay Nakao were in charge of the two checkout stands. Hamburger sold for ten cents a pound, though John sometimes put it on sale for three pounds for a quarter. "People came from all over the island to the store because they liked Johnny's meat," says Kay.

Gross sales were about fifty dollars a week. "Dad was making money hand over fist," Wayne says.

One year later, on December 7, 1941, the Japanese navy bombed Pearl Harbor, decimating the U.S. naval fleet stationed in Hawaii. The United States was at war with Japan, and John's bustling enterprise—indeed, the entire Nakata family's future—was put on hold.

CHAPTER TWO

Launching the Flagship

The Second World War temporarily curtailed the business enterprises of the Nakata and Loverich sons. Mo Nakata and Ed Loverich fought in the war, while other members of the Nakata family were sent to an internment camp in California. When the war ended, John Nakata repurchased Eagle Harbor Market, while Mo and Ed opened another grocery on the island, Bainbridge Gardens. The three men later collaborated in founding Town & Country Market, opposite, in 1957. Right: A 1957 check for $15 from Lou Goller, founder of American Marine Bank, paid to Bainbridge Gardens shortly before Mo and Ed closed its doors to run T&C.

On the morning after the bombing of Pearl Harbor, Pauline Nakata anxiously opened the doors of Eagle Harbor Market. One by one, her colleagues, including her husband, John, and her friend and fellow checker, Kay Nakao, filtered in, trading worried glances and glum expressions. "We were afraid no one would come to shop," Kay Nakao recalls.

The sudden attack by the Japanese navy made for six-inch newspaper headlines across the world. President Franklin Delano Roosevelt called the virtual destruction of the American fleet a "date which will live in infamy." The Nakatas fretted over the potential consequences of the attack on their livelihoods. Neither they nor any other Japanese-American citizens could ever imagine the impact of the war on their lives.

Yet, much to everyone's surprise at Eagle Harbor Market, the store filled up quickly. "People stopped by and bought just one thing to show their support and friendship," says Kay. "It meant so much to all of us."

Like other able-bodied men, Mo Nakata and Ed Loverich were drafted into the military. Each rose through the ranks to become a sergeant. Ed served in the South Pacific with the United States Army Corps of Engineers, and later saw combat in Okinawa. Mo fought with the army's 442nd "Go for Broke" Infantry Regimental Combat Team, composed entirely of Japanese Americans. Recognized as the most highly decorated fighting unit of its size and length of service in the history of the United States military, the 442nd fought in the tall mountains of France and Italy.  Other Bainbridge islanders of Japanese ancestry joined Mo in the 442nd, including Paul Sakai and Arthur Koura, Mo's future brother-in-law.

While these men were willing to fight and die for their country, their families were shamefully uprooted from their homes. Two months after the United States entered the war, President Roosevelt issued Executive Order 9066 mandating an enforced exodus of Japanese Americans to internment camps for the duration of the conflict. Bainbridge Islanders were among the first Japanese Americans to be sent to internment camps, arriving at the Manzanar Relocation Center at the edge of California's Mojave Desert in March 1942. "We had ten days to pack up our things and leave Bainbridge," recalls Jerry Nakata. "One of the Nakao boys told me that when the ferry left the island, my father was on the top deck looking back at Bainbridge with tears in his eyes, thinking he'd never see it again. This was his home. He had lived here for more than forty years."

The Nakatas bid farewell to their farmhouse and strawberry fields. To their undying gratitude, the farm was cared for during the war by the Vadalions, a Filipino family on

the island. The Loveriches also pitched in, offering their private storage places for the Nakatas' possessions, including Jitsuzo's truck, which was stored in their garage. Tom Loverich further watched over the Sakais' land holdings and even buried the family's cash in a container in his backyard.

THE STRENGTH OF FRIENDSHIP

The Loverich and Nakata families stayed in touch during the war, thanks to Hilda Loverich, who exchanged letters with Mo overseas, catching him up on island activities and all the exploits of his buddy Ed. "Haven't heard from [Ed] for quite some time," a worried Mo wrote Hilda in December 1944. "Hope he's OK."

The uncertainties caused by his family's relocation to Manzanar convinced John it was best to sell Eagle Harbor Market. His loyal customers gave him a fitting farewell. "Most had a charge account due," says his son Wayne. "Collecting on each account was a struggle and a challenge at the end of each month, including all the returned bad personal checks. It was very gratifying when Dad's customers . . . all showed up and fully paid off their bills. Even more impressive was that all the bad checks were replaced with good ones."

More than twelve thousand Americans of Japanese ancestry, most of them U.S. citizens born in this country, were imprisoned at Manzanar, ninety miles north of Los Angeles in the agriculturally rich Owens Valley. Another one hundred thousand Japanese Americans met similar fates at other internment camps. The Nakatas didn't let their confinement destroy their spirit. Jitsuzo grew vegetables at the camp and also crafted several items for personal

The Nakata family, above, poses for a portrait at their new "home" at the Manzanar Relocation Center. The family tried as best it could to maintain a semblance of normal life, with Jitsuzo (third from left in the top row) gardening in the rich soil (Manzanar means "apple orchard" in Spanish), and John and his brothers working as butchers. Left of Jitsuzo are his sister Sa and her husband, Joe Kodani; right of Jitsuzo are Pauline, Mo, John, and Ken Nakata. In the bottom row (left to right) are Wayne, Bob, Don, and Shima Nakata. Left: A poster ordering the internment of Japanese Americans on Bainbridge Island.

use, such as chairs and shelving from discarded lumber. When his friend Mr. Murakami passed away, Jitsuzo carved a headstone for his grave.

John Nakata, given his background and experience, supervised the meat cutting in the kitchen and mess hall, assisted by his brothers Jerry and Ken. John's sister Sadako was a nurse's aide in the camp hospital, and Pauline worked as a domestic in the homes of camp administrators. Older women like Shima stayed "home" and cared for the children. Ken graduated from high school at Manzanar and later served in the army.

The young ones were blissfully unaware of their plight, enjoying the camaraderie of the relocation center as if it really was a "camp." As for Jerry, who later joined his sister Jean at an internment camp in Idaho, "all I thought about was Bainbridge Island," he says.

The camps were fenced and patrolled by armed guards. The internees lived in hastily built tar paper–covered barracks of simple frame construction, without plumbing or cooking facilities of any kind. In some cases, the internees were required to build the barracks-like structures themselves. Needless to say, the living conditions were cramped.

Mo and Art Koura were permitted to return to Bainbridge during the war and even visit their families at Manzanar. Art's younger sister Sachiko and Mo had gone to Bainbridge High School together—she was a couple of years behind Mo and used to walk to school with Kay Nakao—and they had struck up a romantic relationship. Extremely bright and literate, Sachiko and her brother Tony were hired by Walt Woodward, editor with his wife, Milly, of the *Bainbridge Island Review* newspaper,

to write dispatches from Manzanar apprising their neighbors of their lives.

In one article, Sachiko wrote of Art's marriage to Florence Yoshitake, commenting that "in the simple ceremony, the bride wore a long, white, silk crepe gown with finger-tip veil and beaded crown."

A VOICE OF REASON

The Woodwards were the only newspaper editors in the country to publicly and strongly criticize the mass internment, and they did so in very personal terms. "It was good to know that Art Koura and Momoichi Nakata were returned for a few days to the place they know as 'home,' even though it is a place they were forced to leave under a national policy which says people related, no matter how remotely, to ONE (and only one) of our enemies must be evacuated," Woodward wrote in an editorial.

He never minced his words, calling the resolution an "abomination" and "asinine," since it excluded American citizens of German and Italian ancestry from the classification of "enemy race." Woodward further reported on the scant but simmering anti-Japanese sentiment on Bainbridge, railing against "hysteria and blind, war-inflamed viewpoints," while upholding the constitutional right of islanders to free speech and assembly.

Art and Mo were both wounded during the war. Sachiko reported, "Sergeant Nakata, Winslow, noted as a basketball player, received slight wounds October 28 [1944], the same day Private Koura was hurt." She was writing of her sweetheart and her brother, respectively. Other dispatches tallied the number of Japanese-American islanders killed in action.

"Sachiko, gal," Woodward wrote in a letter, "don't you miss one damn casualty or death. Let's be sure—you and I—that our Island boys' sacrifices are not in vain."

When Sachiko asked the Woodwards if she should terminate her column, Walt emphatically replied, "No, let's not let the column drop. … Its flame reminds the people of Bainbridge Island and all who care to read the

Jitsuzo spent his time at Manzanar crafting objects for personal use such as this table, left. Made of scrap wood with legs of mesquite or sagebrush, the table is inlaid with Japanese characters that spell out Manzanar, two flowers that, according to Jitsuzo's grandson Wayne Nakata, represent Japan, and a star that stands for America, the country he loved despite the governmental order that incarcerated him and his family.

7:26 AM

TOWN & COUNTRY

Karen Nakata filets the first halibut of the season. Wild-caught Alaskan halibut is delivered to Town & Country Markets' six stores from March to September, and the opening of the season is anticipated weeks ahead.

Mo casually mentioned that the group couldn't spend the rest of their lives making fishing poles. He brought up the grocery business, which all of them had been involved in through the years.

Review that some of our neighbors—our fellow citizens—are living elsewhere temporarily. It is a torch which has burned steadily since a very bad day in December 1941. Don't let its light go out." She didn't.

Mo's wounds were more serious than initially reported. The shrapnel that pierced his leg required a monthlong hospital stay in England. He subsequently was awarded a Bronze Star and Purple Heart for his sacrifices. He had assisted his comrades in rescuing the famed "Lost Battalion" of World War II in the wooded hills of Alsace, France, after the battalion had been trapped for a week. "In the operation, the Nisei lost three times the number of men they rescued," the *Review* reported. The 442nd earned in blood their "Go for Broke" maxim.

On January 2, 1945, the U.S. government rescinded the exclusion order, determining it unconstitutional, and thus allowing the internees to return home and rebuild their lives. Many Japanese Americans had hurriedly sold their farms and businesses prior to their relocation, losing what amounted to substantial sums of money. The Nakatas were more fortunate—although John had lost Eagle Harbor Market, the family retained ownership of the strawberry farm.

Decades would pass before the U.S. government recognized its error. In 1983, Congress finally condemned the internment as "unjust and motivated by racism." Five years later, the government issued an "official apology." In 1988, President Ronald Reagan signed H.R. 442, which authorized financial reparations to the internees to compensate for the damage done to their lives. Today, Manzanar is slowly being transformed into a public historic site. The gravestone Jitsuzo carved for his friend is still standing.

Concerned over lingering racial tensions, Jitsuzo, Shima, and several of their sons, daughters, and their spouses postponed their return home, moving instead to a cabin owned by their friends the Hansens on a ranch in Moses Lake, Washington. "Tub" Hansen also provided much-needed work for John. The Nakatas finally returned to Bainbridge in time for Wayne to enter kindergarten. They would not dwell in the past. Life was for living.

Marriage was in the air. Ed married feisty Billie Sutherland, whose brother, Jack, was killed in the war, and Mo married Sachiko, whom everyone called "Sa." His best man was Ed's brother Francis. In 1946, Mo and Sa welcomed

Mo Nakata and Sachiko Koura, known as "Sa" by her friends, left, were married shortly after the war. While Mo fought, and was subsequently wounded, in Europe, Sa kept Bainbridge Island residents abreast of the news from the front and Manzanar with her contributions to the *Review*.

CHAPTER TWO LAUNCHING THE FLAGSHIP   41

their first son, Larry. Finding work wasn't easy, however. "About the only job Ed, Johnny, Mo, and Jerry could get on the island was wrapping line guides onto bamboo fishing poles for a fellow named Casey Hendricks, who sold them in Canada," says Billie Loverich.

A PARTNERSHIP IS BORN

While sitting there one day in the open-air workshop, Mo casually mentioned that the group couldn't spend the rest of their lives making fishing poles. He brought up the grocery business, which all of them had been involved in through the years. "Mo pointed out that the Bainbridge Gardens grocery store, a thriving business before the war, was now vacant," says Jerry. "He asked John and Ed if they were interested in leasing the place with him, but John declined, thinking the store was too small to support three owners. Big Ed liked the idea, though, and they shook hands on it."

Ed Loverich didn't blink at the prospect of going into business with a Japanese American at a time when some people still harbored prejudices. "There was enough disjointedness left on the island for a few people to . . . advise Ed against his partnership," Woodward wrote in the *Bainbridge Island Review*, "only to get this rejoinder, 'I trust Mo more than any other man I know.'"

Bainbridge Gardens was located in the center of the island at Fletcher Bay. The grocery was next door to a gas station and nursery operated by the Harui family, who also owned the land on which the buildings sat. The partners remodeled the store and kept the name, opening for business in 1947, with Mo cutting the meat while Ed ran the grocery department. Members of their families assisted them: Ken Nakata worked in the meat

Ed Loverich and Mo Nakata opened the Bainbridge Gardens grocery store in 1947. Bainbridge Gardens was originally a produce stand opened in 1912 by Zenhichi Harui and his brother, Zenmatsu Seko. By 1935 Bainbridge Gardens had grown into a large nursery with greenhouses, sunken gardens, and ponds filled with carp. The grocery and a gas station, above, fronted the nursery on Miller Road. Right: Mo Nakata in apron outside the store.

In retirement, longtime friends Jitsuzo Nakata, far left, and Tom Loverich, left, basked in the closeness of their families and the success of their children. In 1949, Jitsuzo lost his wife, Shima, and in 1954 his friend Tom passed away.

department while Mo and Hilda Loverich handled the bookkeeping. Eleven-year-old Wayne Nakata tidied the backyard, and Gary Loverich, just a kid at the time, earned a few pennies straightening out baby food jars.

The store and its neighboring businesses had been a destination point for many years prior to the war, due in no small part to the Harui nursery, which comprised six acres of carefully tended flowers, trees, and other plants. The place flourished and customers' cars lined the stretch of Miller Road that fronted the store. Ed and Mo worked their tails off. "Ed would leave for the store first thing in the morning, come back at five, and then leave again to close the store at eight," Billie Loverich recalls. "He and Mo worked every day, alternating Sundays, and traveling into Seattle by ferry on Mondays to shop for what they needed to buy."

Meanwhile John, joined by his brother Jerry, leased the small Paramount grocery at 15th and Pine Street in Seattle's Capitol Hill neighborhood. Saving every cent, John accumulated enough cash in 1952 to repurchase Eagle Harbor Market, the store he had built in 1940 on the site of the old family home and barbershop. Jerry subsequently took over ownership of the Paramount grocery. The Nakata sons were all gainfully employed, as was their good friend Ed, providing more than a measure of comfort to their parents.

Two island pioneers, Shima Nakata and Tom Loverich, passed away in 1949 and 1954, respectively. With his wife and many friends gone, Jitsuzo spent more time now in the companionship of his grandchildren. Wayne Nakata remembers octopus hunting with Jitsuzo off Blakely Rock, a small island near Eagle Harbor. "We got into his twelve-foot dinghy and were out there pretty far for such a small boat," Wayne recalls. "Grandpa had this long metal bar with a hook on it, and he brought out this thing called a 'bluestone' that looked like mothballs. That was his bait. He put it in a bag at the end of the hook and went to this sizable rock that had a shallow portion with a little pool of water next to it. He said that's where the octopus would be. He fished around with his contraption and within five minutes, up came these big tentacles. We ate fresh octopus that night. To me he was a wizard."

The intrepid adventurer passed away quietly in 1955. Although he did

CHAPTER TWO LAUNCHING THE FLAGSHIP   43

While Mo and Ed enjoyed bustling business at their grocery, Jerry and John Nakata ventured across the Puget Sound to Seattle's Capitol Hill neighborhood and leased the Paramount grocery on 15th and Pine. Left: Jerry (left) and John at the store's counter.

not live to see the next great chapter in the lives of his sons, he was secure in the knowledge that his courage, hard work, and determination had produced a better life for his children.

RIDING THE TIDES OF CHANGE

Bainbridge Gardens and Eagle Harbor Market were successful enterprises. Ed's athletic fame and Mo's effervescent personality and renowned meats combined to make the former a customer destination, while John's quieter demeanor, sensitivity, and longtime reputation as a butcher—in addition to Eagle Harbor's central location—made it thrive as well. But the grocery business was changing. The era of the neighborhood store was drawing to a close. Customers seeking a wider selection of items at less expensive prices gave birth to a new model—the supermarket. Although the retailing concept dates to 1937 when a former employee of Kroger opened a King Kullen in Queens, New York, it didn't catch on nationally until the end of World War II.

Wanting to preserve Winslow as the downtown center, a group of Bainbridge residents and businessmen determined that a supermarket with ample off-street parking could serve as the area's commercial anchor. They incorporated themselves as Bainbridge Investors, Inc. and chose a site for the new market—serendipitously, the empty lot that the Loverich and Nakata boys had played baseball on as children. The group then solicited Ed and Mo's interest in leasing the store. While intrigued, the proposed market's proximity to Eagle Harbor Market gave them pause. They replied that if John were willing to join them, they would give it deep consideration.

When John gave the go-ahead, the three partners pooled their resources to capitalize the island's first supermarket (although an IGA was going up at around the same time). The new store became part of the Thriftway marketing platform created in 1948 by wholesaler

SHARING OUR STORIES

Market Sees Run in Stockings

The Bainbridge Gardens grocery store was located in a long, whitewashed building shaded by a giant willow across the street. Just like the old Eagle Harbor Market, its wooden floors were sprinkled each morning with sawdust, giving the market a homey, old-time feeling—too old in some cases.

Just before the new store was built, a female customer put her foot through a decrepit floorboard and ripped her hosiery. Ed and Mo chipped in and bought her a new pair of stockings.

7:07 AM

TOWN & COUNTRY

David Winter (left) and Fred Harris work the morning's crossword puzzle. For more than a decade, a rotating group of four or five puzzlers has been a weekday morning fixture at the Bainbridge market's coffee shop. They drink coffee, compare crossword solutions, and sometimes delve into heated political debates.

During the grand opening of Town & Country Market on Bainbridge Island, there were so many different activities it was difficult to experience them all. Inside the store, above, children licked ice cream cones and box boy Wayne Nakata hauled a carton of pork & beans, while outside boxers Joe Louis and Max Baer signed autographs in the parking lot, and Stan Boreson dropped wooden coins from a helicopter turning overhead. Left: John Nakata's published thank-you to customers of the Eagle Harbor Market and notice of the upcoming grand opening of T&C.

Associated Grocers (AG). AG provided its member independent retail stores the ability to join together to achieve greater purchasing power, thereby effectively competing against the emerging regional supermarket chains.

Months before the new market was to open, it still did not have a name. Ed and Billie were touring stores in Spokane with a group of other Thriftway owners when a sign over a tire store caught Billie's eye—"Town & Country Tires." She liked the sound of it and brought it to Ed's attention. When they returned to Bainbridge, Ed passed the name along to Mo and John, who agreed it captured the spirit of Winslow—a "town" within the "country." Town & Country Thriftway was born, and the new owners incorporated their company as Town & Country Market, Inc.

THE GRANDEST OPENING

The grand opening on August 29, 1957, is a milestone in the history of Bainbridge Island, an event of such color and magnitude that islanders still talk about it. Waiting for the doors to open, a huge horde assembled outside the modern building—a veritable anachronism on Winslow Way, some of which was still unpaved. On hand was former heavyweight boxing champ Joe Louis. The "Brown Bomber" autographed photos at a table, alongside another heavyweight champ, iron-chinned Max Baer, whom Louis had knocked out in four rounds in 1935. For fun, the boxers feigned antagonism and traded "air" punches.

Stan Boreson, a local television celebrity billed as the "King of Scandinavian Humor," hovered above in a helicopter, dropping wooden tokens that could be redeemed for discounts at T&C and other local businesses. Playing his accordion, Stan later regaled the crowd with favorite tunes like "I Left My Heart in Mukilteo"— sung in Swedish, no less! Meanwhile, Billie and her sister-in-law Elaine Loverich, married to Ed's brother Francis, handed out free ice cream cones. "We dished out more than 1,500 cones," says Elaine. "We counted."

At 10,416 square feet of space, the market was the largest in northern Kitsap County. A thirty-foot-high cedar sign out front broadcast Town & Country (it remains to this day and now

SHARING OUR STORIES

Legendary Boxers Treat Islanders to Signing at Grocery Opening

On August 29, 1957, Town & Country opened its doors to the public on Bainbridge Island for the first time. In the spirit of P. T. Barnum, the event was one big show. For islanders used to a quiet rural existence, the sight of heavyweight boxers Joe Louis and Max Baer landing in a helicopter on Winslow Way must have taken their breath away. "They sat side-by-side just outside the front door, and we all lined up to get an autograph," recalls longtime customer Ralph Munro.

Louis and Baer signed photos of themselves printed next to each other on a 4x6 card. The former heavyweight champs were financially challenged—Louis was hounded by the Internal Revenue Service much of his adult life—and did promotional work to pay their bills. "I can still hear [a fellow] behind me say, 'These guys gave America some of our greatest entertainment, and now the IRS is harassing them, and they have to sit in front of a . . . grocery store and sign autographs to pay their taxes,'" Munro says. "But we all loved our autographs." The fellow behind him gave Louis a hearty handshake "and then leaned over to hug him," adds Munro.

Wayne Nakata was only a boy at the time—a box boy at that, his first job with the company. "Joe Louis was probably the biggest name celebrity ever to come to the island then—maybe ever," he says. "I was so busy I missed most of the entertainment, but I remember when the helicopter started tossing redeemable tokens out to the crowd, and the kids were scrambling around to get them. The store was packed. What a day!"

serves as the community message board). The grand opening merited not one, but two special sections in the *Bainbridge Island Review* and coverage in the *Seattle Times*. One article gushed about the store's automatic doors that opened when a shopper stepped on the floor mat, calling it "magic." "This is more than a new Island building and business," Woodward wrote in an accompanying editorial. "It represents various areas of progressive change and growth for Bainbridge and its inhabitants." As always, Woodward's observations were dead on.

Although T&C was a modern supermarket, it retained the warm, inviting trappings of a family grocery. Mo and John manned the open meat counter under a neon sign reading "Johnny and Moe's Meats," assisted by Sam Nakao, who had secured the Nakata family's purchase of a strawberry farm more than three decades earlier. The open counter gave them the opportunity to interact with customers, and both held court daily. Ed was in charge of groceries, Hilda Loverich was the bookkeeper, Billie's father, Bill Sutherland, was the produce manager, and Ken Nakata was in charge of dairy. Sutherland, who grew organic vegetables at home, often brought them into the store for sale, effectively becoming T&C's first organic farmer. "He loved to grow vegetables, but he didn't particularly care to eat them," laughs Billie.

Wayne Nakata, a senior in high school, was a box boy, decked out in the requisite red vest and black bow tie. His mom, Pauline, probably would have been a checker at the store—joining her pal Kay Nakao at the six checkout stands with the new NCR cash registers that didn't require cranking—were it not for the birth of her and John's son Vernon in 1956. The younger set, comprising Larry Nakata, Gary Loverich, and his kid brother Wayne, cut their teeth as "bottle boys," in charge of the redeemable bottle trade at twenty-five cents an hour. Larry's brother Ronnie, too young for a "real job," he says, swept and pulled weeds in the paved parking lot for a few pennies. "I had to work my way up to bottle boy," Ron laughs.

Don Nakata, John and Pauline's oldest child, missed the grand opening to fulfill his military duties. He had been involved in assisting his father, his Uncle Mo, and Ed in developing the store, and had made the arrangements with Associated Grocers to bring Joe Louis and Max Baer in for the christening. Don was a graduate of Seattle University, where he majored in business and minored in philosophy. He was the first Nakata ever to finish college.

In 1958, Jerry Nakata shuttered the Paramount grocery and worked for a couple of other Seattle-area markets. When Town & Country Market, Inc. acquired a second store in 1960 on the island, Lynwood Market, Jerry signed on to run the produce department. The tiny grocery—it had three employees—was sold in 1968. Jerry laughs that although he made a lot of friends, the store didn't make a lot of money.

Much as the company has been run ever since its inception, the grand opening of T&C was a family affair. Opposite: Billie and Elaine Loverich (left and right, respectively), served ice cream cones to children visiting T&C during the celebration, while their husbands and children helped customers at the checkout lanes and in the aisles. Above: A Medosweet Dairy Foods clock that hung for years behind Johnny and Mo's meat counter.

SHARING OUR STORIES

T&C Reader Board Foregoes Product Promotion for Community Service

Since it was first erected in 1957, the thirty-foot-high cedar sign pylon outside Town & Country on Bainbridge Island has carried many messages for the shoppers, islanders, and visitors traveling down Winslow Way, the commercial center of the island.

At first the sign was used, as were most so-called reader boards, for advertising sale items and new product arrivals. Although it was quite effective as a marketing device, by the 1970s the store was receiving requests from local organizations to utilize the sign for their own announcements. "We made a decision that the sign was more useful for the community to broadcast their messages than for us to point out that canned goods were on sale," says Wayne Loverich.

But by 1975, the market was so deluged with requests from virtually every organization on the island to put up their announcements that it instituted an application policy for island non-profits.

Today, it is common to see announcements about local charity events, island celebrations, and remarkable local achievements, such as when the Bainbridge High School Spartan basketball team made it to the 2007 state finals. "We haven't had a food item on it for more than thirty years!" says Wayne.

One former employee looks back with mixed emotions at the days when food items were advertised on the reader board. Geoff Wilson, who worked at the store from 1968–1973, recalls the time when he was asked to switch out the advertising on the reader board.

"Putting the letters on the sign was fun because you got to scramble up onto the sign and have a bird's-eye view of Winslow Way," says Wilson. He popped his lunchtime pizza bread in the oven—unaware that the oven was already filled with bread crumbs drying for the store's stuffing mix—and clambered up the sign. "Moments later, Pinky [McNulty] ran out of the store and yelled, 'Geoff, did you put something in the oven?' I immediately looked over at the chimney above the oven—it was belching opaque white smoke. Then the siren down at the fire hall went off, and soon I got to watch, like a bird on a wire, as the fire truck raced up to the store to extinguish my cooking. Talk about feeling exposed!"

The stuffing, pizza bread, and oven were a complete loss. Wilson was amazed that he wasn't fired for the incident. Instead, he was moved over to frozen foods where "it was management's belief that I'd have less chance of catching any of the frozen food on fire" and Ed Loverich forever referred to him as "the guy that got me a new oven."

To ensure T&C's success, the owners took very modest salaries, according to Bob Payne, who handled the company's taxes as a partner in the Seattle accounting firm Kelly & Payne. "They worked extremely hard and paid attention to the business," Payne adds. "They knew what they were doing and it paid off, with the store becoming the most popular on the island. People would drive miles to buy John and Mo's meat, which they had aged to perfection. I can still taste it."

COMMUNITY CONNECTIONS

More than meat brought in the crowds. When longtime customer Martha Creech was eight years old in 1958, she and her friends hustled to the store after school to peruse the film schedule located at the checkout stand. "We wanted to see what movies were playing at the Lynwood Theatre," she says, noting that the handout "was promise of the exquisite adventure of Friday Night at the Movies!"

The market was a community nexus, a place to swap stories with fellow islanders and store personnel, chewing the fat about the weather, recent births and deaths, or sports scores. Credit was extended to customers via IOUs signed on the back of the receipt. An unmistakable closeness permeated the place. "In those days, it was OK to pick up the little ones and give 'em hugs," Kay Nakao says. "If a mother checking out forgot to get milk, she'd run to the dairy section while I rocked her baby."

Although now a "bedroom community" to Seattle, Bainbridge still retained its rural character. The island still boasted such small-town charms as a volunteer fire department with a single truck. While the Mosquito Fleet had given way to a modern ferry system, most islanders still knew their captains and crew. Traffic was minimal, and one could leave home for the ferry a few minutes before departure, depending on the distance. "Everybody still knew everybody else," says Billie Loverich.

They not only knew each other, but also had given each other a wild assortment of nicknames. Mo was "Porky" or "Pork Chops," John was "Johnny Butch," and Ed was either "Big Ed" or "Ashcan" to those who remembered his athletic fame. Even customers had odd monikers: Al Davenport, a rather stocky fellow, was called "Porpoise," and longtime customer Mrs. Smith, a local poet and author who arrived at the store at the exact same time every morning, was "Smitty." Family friend Paul Sakai was "Tosh," and Teruo Taniguchi was given the affectionate nickname "Bozo."

Ed had a particular facility with coining nicknames, tagging Larry Nakata with "Lefty," Wayne Loverich with "Wiener," and poor Vern Nakata with "Veronica." "When he didn't know a girl's name, he always called her 'Susie,'" says Vern. "No one knows why." Like other family members, Vern started at the store as a "bottle boy," a difficult proposition for a boy who didn't like bees. "They'd swarm around the bottles because of the sugar in them," he explains. "I always kept a can of Raid with me."

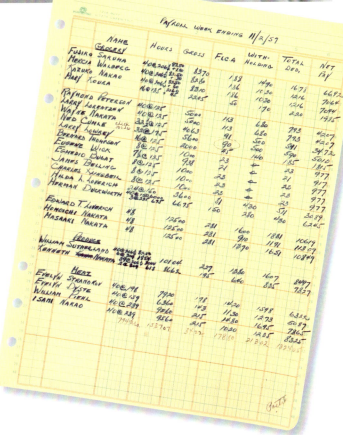

Kay Nakao, above, met Mo and Ed in high school. Later, when the two men operated Bainbridge Gardens, Kay helped run the checkout stands. When T&C opened, Kay found a home at "Old Number One," the checkout stand she would work at for the next twenty-five years. Right: A page from T&C's payroll from November 1957 indicates the owners' hours worked and pay rates, a modest sum for the times.

8:30 AM

GREENWOOD MARKET

Produce clerk Marcus Klausenburger restocks lemons. Greenwood Market serves as the neighborhood market for the community north of downtown Seattle, and is frequented by stay-at-home parents, senior citizens, and workers throughout the day.

SHARING OUR STORIES

Produce Clerk Saves Day with Cookie Recipe

Town & Country, as every Bainbridge Islander knows, is far more than a supermarket. It's a place to connect with friends, a meeting place before heading off to dinner or a movie, and, for longtime customer Kathleen Horne, an irreplaceable source of information in desperate times.

Late one evening shortly after the giant retail chain Safeway set up shop on the island, "I was baking cookies for an event the following day, using a very complicated and ingredient-intensive recipe found on the back of a bag of gourmet-style chocolate chips," Kathleen recalls. "I was in the middle of the process when the recipe suddenly disappeared! I searched the countertops, floor, and trash in vain. Desperate, I phoned T&C. Since it was close to midnight, only the produce clerk was on the floor."

Frantically, Kathleen explained her crisis. The clerk "good-naturedly walked over to the baking aisle, found a bag of the chips, and read the entire recipe to me over the phone," she says.

"I still have the recipe and remain a loyal T&C fan."

Ed also ran a nickel and dime sports betting pool at the market for workers and customers. "He'd walk the aisles with a transistor radio in his pocket and this wire that went into his earpiece to hear the scores," says Gary Loverich. "People thought he was hard of hearing."

The store boasted entertainment beyond movie times and betting pools. Jack Ancich, who also had a nickname—"the fish guy"—came to T&C's parking lot every Friday and hawked seafood from his truck. Blocks away, pedestrians could hear Jack's inimitable pitch, "It's a show, Missus! It's a show!" Then, there was Russ Monroe, a customer who enjoyed few things more than coming into the store first thing in the morning and belting songs on the microphone used for announcements. And he wasn't half bad!

By the mid-1960s, much had changed on Bainbridge Island during its journey from a lumber and shipbuilding mecca to a bedroom community to Seattle. Winslow Way, above, while changed drastically from the early days when Tom Loverich guided his Ford Model T over its heavy ruts, looks much the same today, to the delight of long-time locals.

The Nakatas offered cooking lessons at the Commodore School on Bainbridge, where their sukiyaki dinners were a big hit and raised money for the schools. The antagonism toward Japanese Americans had largely dissipated, due in no small part to the mixed racial backgrounds of T&C's owners and the particular closeness of their families and other store personnel. "There was a gentleman who was very anti-Japanese and had written nasty letters to the newspaper during the war," says Kay Nakao. "He used to shop in the store with his wife. I promised myself, 'Kay, you are going to win this man over even if it takes you a year to do it.' It didn't take nearly that long. I treated him so nicely, just like I do everyone else, that he soon let go of his prejudices."

A FAMILY AFFAIR

As the years progressed, more family members found jobs at the company. Elaine Loverich joined T&C's new bakery in 1965, and later assisted her sister-in-law Hilda in the bookkeeping department. Larry Nakata worked on weekends during the school year and full-time during the summers to pay for his tuition at Olympic College in Bremerton, then at the University of Washington, graduating from the latter with a degree in urban development from the school of business. During his senior year, he married his high school sweetheart, Sandy Naylor, then left T&C in 1969 to serve several years in the army in Washington, D.C.

The same year, Ron Nakata took a full-time job at T&C as a grocery clerk stocking shelves, while Ed and Billie's daughter Christy worked part-time summers cooking rotisserie chickens for Mo. Their nephew Wayne Loverich worked summers as a box boy until graduating from Bainbridge High School in 1964. He attended junior college in Aberdeen, and then spent three years in the army, including nine months in Vietnam, before leaving the service as an infantry first lieutenant. Wayne returned to T&C in 1971.

Of all the family members to join the family business, none was more crucial than Don Nakata. After his military service, Don returned to T&C full-time, assisting Ed on the grocery side and gradually taking over more responsibility. "Ed was easygoing and he saw a lot of good points about Don, who was just so smart and optimistic," says Jerry.

Don had met his future wife, Ellen, during a trip to Hawaii in 1960. Ellen was working at a local travel agency when Don came in to book a bicycle tour. He needed a date for a luau that evening and asked Ellen to join him. The two hit it off and launched a long-distance courtship. Serendipity then intervened to put the couple in closer proximity.

Ellen's childhood ambition was to become a stewardess. She was hired by Pan American Airways and trained in New York City. "There were two openings in Seattle, and we had to draw straws," she

> Of all the family members to join the family business, none was more crucial than Don Nakata. "Ed saw a lot of good points about Don, who was just so smart and optimistic," says Jerry Nakata.

Don Nakata pictured above (right) with a fellow soldier in the U.S. Army, was the first member of his family to attend and graduate from college. Don, who missed T&C's grand opening because of his military obligations, brought modern business sensibilities to the company.

SHARING OUR STORIES

Town & Country Meat Scale Does Double Duty

Back in the days when Town & Country had the only paved parking lot on the island, it also had something else—the only reliable weighing scale. "Everyone took items to the store to have them weighed," says Ralph Munro, who has shopped at the store for much of his life.

The scale was in the back of the store where John Nakata and his brother Mo cut meat in between gabbing with customers, an activity both men enjoyed. The sign above said, "Johnny and Moe's Meats," but it might as well have said, "Free and Accurate Weighing of Anything Under a Hundred Pounds."

"It was the only decent scale on the island," Munro explains. People weighed the usual fare like potatoes and a leg of lamb, as well as rather atypical items. "Sometimes people took in their babies to check their weight," Ralph says.

These days the scale no longer is used to weigh infants. Not that the store would mind.

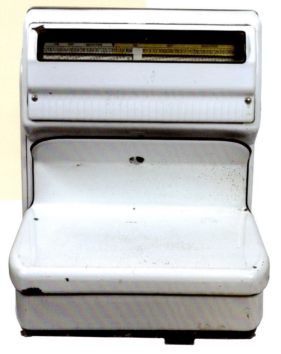

says. "One of the gals who got the Seattle slot wanted to be able to travel home to England where her family lived, so she preferred the New York base, which I had drawn. I felt sorry for her so I traded, which allowed me to be closer to Don."

From the new Seattle-Tacoma International Airport, Ellen flew regular 707 flights to Alaska during the summer months. In the fall of 1961, Ellen transferred to Honolulu to fly international routes, which fulfilled her dream of seeing the world. In 1962, because stewardesses couldn't be married, she hung up her wings and married Don, settling down to family life. The newlyweds' first child, Susan, was born in 1965. A second daughter, Julie, followed in 1967.

Three years later, Don purchased some shares in Town & Country Market, Inc. from his father, John, who was pulling back from work at the store. In 1971, following John's official retirement, Don purchased the remainder of his father's shares. When Mo suffered a near-fatal heart attack in 1971, Don became more of a force at the company. Mo had successfully diversified into real estate over the years, and had even created a novel profit-sharing plan for T&C employees that included real estate assets. "Like Don, Mo was an idea person, and he and Don fed off each other," says CPA Payne. "But Don was the one with the business degree. He brought with him more modern ideas—next generation ideas. He was a visionary."

Inspired by Mo, Don took Town & Country Market, Inc. to the next stage, opening a second supermarket on the island in partnership with William Hoffman and Louis Peltier, two former Associated Grocers executives. Called Village Foods, the market occupied a former IGA store that had moved across the street. The venture marked a turning point for the organization: interest in growing beyond the successful foundation store on Winslow Way. This risky expansion strategy would be carried into the future by Don Nakata, firmly planting him as the company's leader.

The three founders of T&C, John Nakata, Mo Nakata, and Ed Loverich, were fortunate in having a family member capable of taking their company through its next stage—John's son Don. Above: A portrait of the four men (left to right): Don, Mo, Ed, and John.

CHAPTER THREE

Uncharted Waters

Don Nakata cast his eye beyond Bainbridge Island in seeking a location for Town & Country Market, Inc.'s newest supermarket. He settled on the picturesque town of Poulsbo, a largely rural area of small farms and budding subdivisions, twelve miles away on the Kitsap Peninsula.

The energy crisis was in full throttle following the Arab oil embargo of 1973, plunging the nation into economic recession. Gasoline prices soared into the stratosphere, pinching consumer wallets and causing long lines at service stations. To appeal to shoppers' budget-consciousness, Associated Grocers introduced a discount grocery concept called Mark-It Foods, and Don decided the new supermarket would subscribe to this model. "It was the company's first big expansion, and if it went right, Don felt the company would just keep growing," says Wayne Nakata.

The no-frills Mark-It model helped owners operate on a shoestring budget. Each store was enclosed in a plain warehouse environment. Goods were stacked on cement floors. There were minimal promotions, and customers took upon themselves the task of finding merchandise and marking the price on an item with a grease pencil—the origin of the concept's name. They also bagged their groceries and carried them out. The savings in labor and other operating expenses were passed on to shoppers in the form of reduced prices. "Every aisle is filled with items priced way below fancy conventional supermarkets," advertisements proclaimed. "We buy in big quantities at big discounts and pass the savings along to you. And every item is backed by our 100% quality guarantee."

Each owner of a Mark-It store got to pick its name. Poulsbo was composed largely of Scandinavians—the town's unofficial nickname is "Little Norway"—prompting Larry Nakata's wife, Sandy, to suggest Viking Mark-It Foods. The other partners liked the name, but they were less certain the venture would prove a success. "It was a big stretch, but Don was determined and brave enough to go for it," says Vern Nakata. The store opened for business in 1974.

Despite its austerity, Viking Mark-It Foods enjoyed the same convivial feel as T&C on Bainbridge. Built on land homesteaded by Clarence and Gladys Paulson, it was a warm, welcoming place, and the community gravitated toward it. Store personnel were on a first-name basis with shoppers like Gladys, the official first customer. It was not uncommon for the deli to welcome first-time shoppers with a free half-pound of sliced meat and a half-pound slab of cheese. As the *North Kitsap Herald* noted in a profile, "a spirit of friendliness and service . . . and small town values . . . prevailed."

Don managed the new store with Bob Reister, leaving T&C in the capable hands of Ed Loverich and his nephew Wayne Loverich. Other Nakatas moved over to Viking Mark-It: Jerry managed the produce department, Don's wife, Ellen, signed on as bookkeeper, and Larry Nakata worked in the grocery department with Mike Davis, the assistant manager, when not backing up Jerry in produce. "Don put all he had into this store," says Ellen. "And it grew very rapidly."

Expansion was the overriding theme of Don Nakata's tenure heading up Town & Country Market, Inc. New stores would proliferate beyond Bainbridge Island. The Ballard Market, opposite, in Seattle exemplified the kind of store Don envisioned—convivial, community-oriented, quality-focused, and a place where shopping was fun. Don's first new store, Viking Mark-It in Poulsbo, initially was predicated on a discount format, whereby customers wrote the prices of items on the goods with a grease pencil, right.

> "What really made the company stand out among the 177 independent retailers we had back then were its employees. They were worlds apart from their contemporaries, and that is a strong statement," says Art Jones, retired president of Associated Grocers.

The store's success is attributable to Don's business acumen, timing, and people skills. His personal integrity and profound love of people defined the place, and many employees felt they were part of his extended family. "Don always had an intuitive sense of the local market scene and tremendous sensitivity to what people wanted," says Art Jones, retired president of Associated Grocers. "What really made the company stand out among the 177 independent retailers we had back then were its employees. They were worlds apart from their contemporaries, and that is a strong statement."

Personalized customer service was Don's touchstone. "Every customer is a human being and shall be treated with dignity, courtesy, and respect," he wrote in the new store's employee handbook. "All customers will be politely greeted and sincerely thanked for shopping with us. Whenever possible, a customer shall be greeted by name. Every complaint will be treated as an opportunity to gain or retain a loyal customer. Our customers always come first."

CHANGING OF THE GUARD

As Viking Mark-It took off, T&C on Bainbridge was changing. John Nakata retired in 1972 and sold the remainder of his ownership shares in Town & Country Market, Inc. to Don, who now owned a one-third interest in the company. Ed was beginning to pull back as the store's manager while giving Wayne Loverich more responsibility for managing the store on a daily basis, and Mo Nakata was branching out further into his real estate ventures.

Since its 1957 grand opening, T&C had put its heart and soul behind the community's needs, sponsoring a wide array of charitable and philanthropic activities, and as the new generation took

Viking Mark-It Foods in Poulsbo, left, was a reaction to the austerity caused by the oil crisis of the 1970s. Consumers struggled with double-digit inflation, long lines at gas stations, and great political uncertainty. The store offered shoppers a way to lower their grocery bills by taking on tasks normally reserved for employees. It also sold atypical merchandise like shoes and offered services like film processing, along with customary merchandise like produce, seafood, and meat. But, what invited shoppers back time and again was the market's central role in their community.

over from the founders, that spirit of community and dedication to customer service remained. When a customer died, Mo would drive to the person's home to deliver a ham to the customer's family, his way of expressing his condolences. If a customer called on the phone for an item the store did not have, a member of the staff bought it at another market and had it ready when the shopper arrived—modeling Ed's example. The bond between the staff and their fellow islanders was as inextricable as the store's ties to the island.

In the late 1970s, the Bainbridge store took inspiration from a Thriftway promotion and launched an annual themed event that became an institution not only for the grocery store, but for all Winslow merchants: Hawaiian Days. For two weeks, the store was decorated with palm trees and Hawaiian flowers,

Ed Loverich, above, would listen to a transistor radio whenever there was a game on, so shoppers would often ask him the score when they weren't discussing items they would like the store to carry. Left: The red apron worn by T&C employees throughout the 1950s.

SHARING OUR STORIES

Ed Goes Distance for Customers

Ed Loverich just hated it when a customer asked for an item that Town & Country didn't have. He hated it so much that it stuck in his craw, nagging him on business trips to other markets and on vacations, where he visited stores to scrutinize the merchandise on the shelves. "My father would go anywhere to get anything for anybody," says Christy Loverich.

In the years before Safeway came to Bainbridge Island, a customer happened to mention to Ed that he had bought a particular brand of white hominy at the chain store and wished T&C carried it. Ed could just not let go of the memory. "He was in a Safeway on a vacation in California, and remembered the customer's comment," Christy recalls. "He brought a full case home on the plane."

On another occasion, a regular shopper mentioned she had been to a market in Bremerton and purchased a granola blend that she found delicious. Ed hopped in his car and drove to Bremerton to buy it. Another time a woman who wanted to make gooseberry pie was disappointed when the store ran out of gooseberries. Ed went to the Pike Place Market and picked some up. "He'd go buy these items and never mark them up, selling them at cost," Christy notes. "His customers were the world to him."

2:04 PM

SHORELINE CENTRAL MARKET

Meat cutter Marjorie Kori trims steaks, tossing the usable scraps into a bin for ground beef and the remainder into a waste bin. Meat cutting is an exacting trade, and T&C's meat cutters typically bring their own set of knives to the job.

and store personnel wore Hawaiian shirts, skirts, and muumuus. Ed donned a costume and giant headdress as King Kamehameha the Great, the conqueror of the Hawaiian Islands at the turn of the nineteenth century. The elaborate, yellow, foot-high headdress made Big Ed the tallest person on the island, and he didn't shy away from the attention. "For a quiet man, Ed was a bit of a ham," confesses his wife, Billie.

Ed took great pleasure in leading the annual Fourth of July parade down Winslow Way on a float built by produce manager Bill Maier and other staff. Ed was accompanied by bare-chested male employees tooting conch shells and female employees in sarongs dancing the hula. Among them was bookkeeper Elaine Loverich. "I had a group of about ten or so gals with me, and we all took lessons—we were a serious hula dancing group," she says. Each summer, Ed and Billie hosted an event for employees called the "Salmon Derby," whereby staff competed in a fishing tournament. "We'd start in the morning and fish all day," recalls Susan Calhoun, a T&C checker at the time. "Then we'd all go to Ed and Billie's house on the water and have a big picnic on their deck, followed by prizes for who caught the biggest fish."

EXPLORING NEW TASTES

In the early 1980s, Wayne took steps to differentiate T&C from the other island store and its sister store in Poulsbo. "Customers would come in and say, 'Wayne, how come I can buy Corn Flakes fifteen cents a box cheaper at Viking Mark-It?'" he says. "I'd explain that Mark-It was a discount store. I mentioned to Don once that customers were comparing

SHARING OUR STORIES

Island Days Tradition Transforms Store into Tropical Paradise

One day, Town & Country checker Susan Calhoun magically turned Ed Loverich into Hawaii's King Kamehameha. This transformation was for the annual Fourth of July parade down Winslow Way. The store's staff had come up with an idea they called "Hawaiian Days" in which they all dress up in the garb of native Hawaiians. Ed and Billie Loverich loved Hawaii, so convincing Ed to don a foot-tall headdress and Billie to wear a muumuu was pretty easy. "I said to Ed, 'Why not let a young guy do it?' and he said, 'No way, I'm going to play that part,'" Billie recalls.

Ed turned to Susan, who is something of a seamstress, for assistance in designing and building his costume. At six-feet two-inches tall, Ed required a lot of cloth, she says. "I also was in charge of designing the big float we did for the parade," Susan adds. "It was on a flatbed truck, and it was beautifully decorated. Several gals from the store wore sarongs. As a matter of fact, so did Ken Nakata, although his looked something like a diaper. He was bare chested, and I can still see him blowing on that conch shell, making this 'whoooo' sound, while the rest of us passed out candy. It took off from there, and eventually the whole island went Hawaiian."

Indeed, so impressive was the store's theme that other local businesses got into the act and called the annual event "Island Days." Each Independence Day they competed for the title of Best Decorated Store. Three times T&C took home the prize. One year, a Hawaiian friend of Ed and Billie's showed up for the event and testified to its authenticity. "We had a talent show, and I remember the fellow's wife played the ukulele while their kids danced. We set up a little stage for them in the store next to where the dog food is, clearing it out so they could perform during certain times of the day."

Like all good things, Island Days came to an end. "It just ran its course," Susan says. "After our remodeling in 1989, we had a strawberry theme that commemorated the island's strawberry farming history. We all wore aprons with strawberry logos on them and these hats that were green and red to look like a real strawberry, but it just wasn't the same."

Wayne Loverich, near left, was the longtime store director at Town & Country on Bainbridge Island and currently sits on the board. He was instrumental in bringing a wide array of gourmet foods to the store, setting T&C even farther apart from its nearest competitors. Far left: Ken Nakata photographed in 1984, had been with T&C for more than thirty years.

prices. He had a grin on his face as he raised his hands and said nothing. I caught his drift—there was nothing we could do about our prices, so we had to make things different."

Soft-spoken and reserved, Wayne dynamically pushed the envelope on the market's evolution, especially in the items it sold. Like Ed, he listened to customers' requests and did his best to meet them. And he encouraged the staff to do the same. "One of the most remarkable things about the store was the support I always got to give customers what they wanted—to go out and find products they requested," says Margaret Clark, a produce clerk at T&C in the 1980s.

To distinguish the store, Wayne and the staff ordered specialty foods like Bon Maman jams from France, certified Angus beef, free-range chicken, natural pork, and gourmet mustards. Ken Nakata, the dairy manager, brought in specialty cheeses, becoming the store's first cheese expert. Don previously had developed a customer request form for the Poulsbo store, and Wayne incorporated it at the Winslow store. He also provided space in the parking lot out back for aluminum can recycling. Gradually, T&C became known for its variety of specialty goods. The strategy was a winner. "Product lines expanded, price sensitivity declined, and value surfaced," says Wayne, a stockholder since 1989 and today the company's director of food service operations. "We found the niches that would take us into the future."

Still, satisfying customer tastes was only part of the store's community appeal. "Many shoppers told me that T&C was the social event of their day, the place they came to meet and talk to friends as they bumped into them with their baskets," says checker Kay Nakao.

Ed and Billie Loverich's daughter Christy, above right, shown at a Hawaiian Days picnic, started like most family members at Town & Country—stocking shelves as a teen. Christy later went on to organize and manage the floral department at T&C. Above left: Kay Nakao, a longtime friend and employee of the Loverich and Nakata families, celebrating Hawaiian Days with the customers she always enjoyed the most—children.

In 1982, on her twenty-fifth anniversary at T&C, Kay hung up her apron for the last time. She had begun her long affiliation with the Nakata family at the Bainbridge Gardens store, and her husband, Sam, had assisted John and Mo in the meat department since T&C's grand opening. "I was feted at a retirement party with cake and coffee in the back room, and many customers came by to wish me well," Kay recalls. "Afterwards, I went back to my stand, Old Number One, and continued working my shift, but all afternoon I just sobbed. And when I got home, I was so choked up I couldn't eat dinner. Sam said, 'Kay, everyone else goes out smiling and you're the one that cries.' I just loved that store."

T&C continued its modern evolution, adding customer-driven provisions like an espresso bar located in an outside tent with chairs and tables, and a fresh flower market positioned in another tent, overseen by Christy Loverich, manager of the floral department, which flourished under her care. Christy became the head of the floral department under unusual circumstances. In 1985 Don and Ellen Nakata visited Europe with about thirty other Thriftway store owners, including Don's friend Dick Rhodes, then the owner of the Queen Anne Thriftway. The trip was organized so that the store owners could visit manufacturers around the continent, and the first stop on the trip was the Aalsmeer Flower Auction in Amsterdam. A few weeks after the trip, Dick returned to Europe with a smaller group of Queen Anne Thriftway associates to place orders at some of the places he had visited. At the Amsterdam flower auction, Dick ordered what he thought was a manageable container of flowers to sell back at home. Instead, a truck-sized container filled with pallets and pallets of cut flowers was bound for Seattle.

"Dick called Don and said, 'I am in a bind: how am I going to get rid of all these flowers?'" recalls Ellen. Don stepped in to help his friend out, taking three pallets of flowers—a whopping one thousand bunches of cut flowers.

"Huge quantities arrived and I was the only female working in the produce department at T&C so I was assigned to deal with it," says Christy. When the flowers arrived, they were already sweating from the long journey from Europe, and the company had only one day to get them all out for sale at the Bainbridge store. "We rounded up every bucket, pail, and garbage can that would hold water to display all the flowers at the checkout stands," recalls Christy. "They sold like crazy. What started out as a big mistake turned into the beginning of fresh-cut flower sales at the company."

The robust earnings from T&C and Viking Mark-It gave the company the financial wherewithal to buy the T&C site in 1982. Meanwhile, the small Village Foods market, while not a big earner, held its own. Ron Nakata managed the produce department at the market and did with produce what Wayne had done with groceries. He introduced a broader menu of fresh fruits and vegetables, some new to islanders' taste buds. He also was a veritable Picasso when it came to exhibiting produce, harmonizing their colors in mouth-watering displays.

Through the 1980s, many company personnel traveled abroad to Europe and Asia, or domestically throughout the states, in search of better products, new markets, and innovative marketing and promotional concepts. Christy looked for exotic flowers or bargain deals on quality roses, Wayne sampled deli items from New York's famed Zabar's and Harrods department store in London, while Don, who took numerous trips as a member of AG's board of directors, scoped each store's layout, work flow, and merchandise. "On vacations, all we did was look at stores," laughs Susan Allen, Don and Ellen's daughter.

Village Foods closed for business in 1985 upon the loss of the lease. Town & Country Market, Inc. now had two stores under its umbrella, each evolving. Viking Mark-It had changed with the times and had a new name—Poulsbo Market Place. The recession was long over and the store's discount strategy lost its appeal. More important, the supermarket chain Albertsons moved into the area. Don and Larry, the store's directors, coined a phrase, "quiet confidence," to describe the challenge ahead. They put full faith in their employees and the remodeled operation.

MARKET TO MARKET PLACE

The term "market place" essentially defined the store's new strategy, signifying fresh produce, meat, and seafood. The concept was spawned by downtown Seattle's famed Pike Place Market, which featured local produce, flowers, freshly off-the-boat fish, and high quality meats sold by vendors in stalls. "There's an equation that we often use in our business," Don said in announcing the new strategy. "'Price plus Quality equals Value.'" He added that "focusing on price only can be very dangerous, for price without quality is no value at all."

SHARING OUR STORIES

T&C Tailors Holiday Program to Benefit Local Charity

In the 1970s, the Town & Country Market on Bainbridge Island adopted a marketing concept developed by Associated Grocers' Thriftway program called the Turkey Punch Card. The purpose of the program was to give shoppers a way to rack up points to receive a free turkey by buying food and other merchandise. "We'd credit people beginning about eight weeks before Thanksgiving for the dollar amount of groceries they bought," explains Wayne Loverich. "For every $500 they bought with the Turkey Card, we would give credit comparable to a free turkey."

The rules were pretty strict, and many customers would get close to the free turkey and just miss out—not the nicest message to convey around the holidays. "We began telling people that if they spent $200, we'd take that and convert it into credit for a turkey and then donate the cost of the turkey to Helpline House, an organization on the island that helps people in need," Wayne recalls. "It took off big time, with most shoppers using the card for charity. One year I remember we gave $15,000 to Helpline."

The program continues today, though T&C no longer is part of the Thriftway platform. "Each year we at the store and our community of shoppers feel great to provide what is a considerable amount of money from the Turkey Card to Helpline House," Wayne says. "It's really what Thanksgiving is all about."

It is the company's philosophy "to give back to the community that gives so much to us," says Larry Nakata. At all its stores, whether it's sponsoring the local Little League, giving a percentage of sales to non-profit organizations, running for a cure for breast cancer, or donating to the Food Bank—the list goes on and on—the company can be relied on for help.

1:03 AM

POULSBO CENTRAL MARKET

James Jensen uses a pallet jack to place cases of merchandise along the aisles for restocking. Although Poulsbo Central Market is open around the clock, a team of stockers works from pallets during the early morning hours to have the shelves stocked for the next morning's customers.

Greg Johnson (right, speaking with sports radio personality Wayne Cody) was instrumental in bringing T&C into the computer age. His computer and electronic savvy revolutionized not only how the company sold groceries at the point of sale, but also how they managed their overall business. These changes helped the company make their next big expansion.

In 1984, Ron Nakata came over to the renamed store to assist Uncle Jerry in the produce department, applying his artistry to the task. He joined a young man named Greg Johnson, whom Jerry had hired in 1977. Greg had studied to be a shop teacher and had earned a degree in industrial engineering, supporting himself by working for Albertsons. He put his carpentry talents to work for Jerry, building a checkout stand and a floral enclosure. Greg was then asked to assist the store with developing its information technology. Point-of-sale computers using electronic scanning equipment to identify barcoded items and their prices had just been developed. Given Greg's abilities, Don asked him to manage a project to replace the Poulsbo store's cash registers with the new system.

The scanners improved overall productivity, and the captured data was a treasure trove of information. Greg also programmed the company's first automated spreadsheets, dusted off its first personal computers, and introduced scanners to the other stores. Each project provided valuable insight into his next technological endeavor. "There was no one in the nation doing what Greg was doing, and Don was so proud of him," says Vern Nakata.

Poulsbo Market Place was a huge success, thanks to the support of the community, which made it their town hall. "We were the place where people came to shop, visit, and connect with neighbors, friends, and family," says Tom Hall, who worked as a night stocker at the store in the early 1980s and later became the store director.

"This connection with the community was meaningful and powerful. We were involved in area schools and community organizations, and many kids in the county got their first jobs working here as stockers. They'd come back fifteen years later and say, 'I used to work here as a teenager, and it changed my life. Here is where I learned my basic values and work ethic.'"

When customers shopped at the store and found they had forgotten their wallets, "we'd say, 'No problem. Just pay us when you come back next time,'" Tom says. "At our heart, we were still the old neighborhood grocery."

With Village Foods gone, Don now mulled the operation of another store, this time east of the Puget Sound. A well-known chain of markets, Lucky Stores, had foundered in the state, and Associated Grocers had picked up the option on its twenty-six stores. Don joined several other AG members on a tour of the markets. Of the lot, only one, in the working-class neighborhood of Ballard in Seattle, appealed to him. The other retailers were surprised, finding the Ballard location wanting. It was run-down, looked like a drugstore rather than a market, and had been a weak performer for Lucky. Always the visionary, Don saw something they didn't.

Like Poulsbo, Ballard was home to many Scandinavian Americans, whose ancestors worked in its shipyards and fisheries, finding the area reminiscent of home. Don liked the people of Ballard, their work ethic and values, and imagined the store could be a community gathering place like Poulsbo Market Place and T&C. He had met an AG executive named Bill Weymer who was interested in the retail grocery business. The two men decided to combine their talents in leasing the Ballard store in 1985. "Bill and my father thought alike and had a similar makeup," says Susan Allen.

Town & Country Market, Inc. formed a separate subsidiary called Excellence in Food Marketing to accommodate the partnership. "Our goal was to transform the store into a community-focused market that was centered around the concept of fresh food," says Weymer, today the president of Cascade Dafo Inc., a manufacturer of custom leg braces for children.

Following substantial remodeling that included a doubling in the size of its produce department, the renamed store, Ballard Market, opened. Its location at the bottom of a hill had been a problem for the previous owners, and to raise the store's profile, Don and Weymer determined it required a large sign. "At the time, giant vinyl awnings

Poulsbo Market Place was a huge success, thanks to the support of the community, which made it their town hall. "We were the place where people came to shop, visit, and connect with neighbors, friends, and family," says Tom Hall, who later became the store director.

With the economic recovery of the late 1970s and early 1980s, the discount format of the Viking Mark-It gave way to the Poulsbo Market Place, right, offering customers a more modern shopping experience. Despite the change, the community's relationship with the store did not alter, and the store became famous for unique events and promotions.

Where previous tenants had struggled, Ballard Market, top, became a stunning success, partly due to its immense awning. The awning featured a sailboat, which reflected Ballard's maritime history but soon became the logo for the whole T&C organization. Above: A wooden sailboat from a Ballard Market display case.

with lights underneath were all the rage," Weymer says. "So we built this massive red, white, and blue awning that stretched the entire length of the building. The company that made it for us said it was the biggest sign in Seattle."

A SYMBOL SETS SAIL

The awning featured the store name and something else—the sailboat that Don had drawn in defining the company's mission. Don and Weymer had been thinking about distilling the company's mission and values via a compelling graphic image and a few key words. "Don had already explicated these themes in narrative form, but wanted a symbol that conveyed them in shorthand," says Weymer. Don had read author Tom Peters' *In Search of Excellence* and was impressed by Peters's description of the three sides of a successful business, which he'd depicted as a triangle. In 1986, in a meeting with the Associated Grocers advertising team, Don and Weymer were presented with some potential logos, one of which was a sailboat. "The image drew on Ballard's nautical history," Weymer explains. "Don was taken in by the notion of 'sailing one's own ship,' which tied into his strategy of each company store's independence."

The logo, which broke the sailboat graphically into three constituent parts—the two sails and the hull—was given the green light. Subsequently, Don adapted his business principles to the

SHARING OUR STORIES

Customers Dance, Bowl, Date in the Aisles at Ballard Market

When Ballard Market opened in 1985, it set a standard for entertainment in the neighborhood that has yet to be surpassed, chic restaurants and hip bars of the present day excluded. The store's staff was a highly creative bunch that took great pleasure in conjuring unforgettable events for customers.

"Singles Night" was their first creation, a way for single folk in the area to meet in an unusual setting—a supermarket. There, amid boxes of detergent and a potpourri of produce, men and women could strike up conversations about the health properties of okra or the stain-removing potential of Tide. The store also used the occasion to demo specialty products. Back in 1895, Ballard was know as the "Shingle Capital of the World" for manufacturing more shingles than anywhere else in the region. Nearly one hundred years later, the store's staff was working to make it the "Singles Capital of the World."

After the fire department closed down the second Singles Night because of overcapacity issues—"the place was jammed to the rafters because of the event's popularity," says store director Steve Williams—the creative minds at Ballard Market seized on a new idea—"Cruz Nite." Disco, after all, was dead, and the music of the 1950s (Anyone remember Sha Na Na?) was experiencing a nostalgic revival. Employees and customers donned leather jackets and poodle skirts, the men slicking back their hair into ducktails. It was not uncommon to see a couple of old-timers Lindy to Elvis Presley's "Blue Suede Shoes." Their events were a big deal for the area, drawing in customers, neighbors, and even the media. "At this store we've always believed our job is to nurture relationships with the community," Williams says.

image. "Next to the leading sail he put the words, 'satisfying customer wants and needs,'" Weymer says. "Next to the back sail or follow sail, he wrote, 'creativity and innovation.' And next to the hull, which he referred to as the foundation, he wrote, 'people.' The philosophy he wanted to communicate was that you satisfy customer needs through creativity, innovation, and respect for people. It was a great way to add meaning to the logo."

Don also comprehended the metaphorical value of the sailboat. "He loved finding new ways to express the potential of the sailboat to employees, through concepts like 'guiding your own ship,' and 'keeping your hands on the tiller' and being the 'captain of your own ship,'" Weymer says. "Once we had that logo, the philosophy really came together in a big way. Don had distilled the company's purpose in a very meaningful way."

The awning became a beacon for the Ballard community. "I was driving home once listening to my car radio when I heard the weatherman, who was flying in a helicopter above, say, 'Folks, I'm flying over Ballard now, and there is a new landmark below,'" Weymer says. "'I can see it here in red, white, and blue, and it says the Ballard Market.' I about drove off the bridge."

While the awning brought shoppers to the store, what made them come back again and again was their experience. "Don established a link between the store and the community," says Steve Williams, who has worked at Ballard Market since its inception and today is the store director. "He wanted it known in the community as a good neighbor, someone to support schools, churches, and community groups. It's been a love affair ever since."

Weymer agrees. "It wasn't the changes to the exterior and interior that made the store successful," he says. "Our employees were special folks, people like Steve Williams, and 'Gabby' and Steve Curtis. They engaged customers personally. They cared about them. And they were just plain committed to making the store work."

Taking a page from T&C's Hawaiian Days celebration, this creative group invented "Singles Night at the Ballard Market," which soon became the most

Employees at T&C on Bainbridge have kept up the tradition of marching in the annual Fourth of July parade down Winslow Way. A highlight for islanders is the T&C theme, which changes each year. In 1995, the theme was 1957, replete with Mickey Mouse ears and hula hoops, above, while in 2004 employees, including Karin Beran and Gwen Billings (holding the banana) took part in the whimsical "Going Bananas" theme, left.

talked-about event in Seattle. "We were trying to drum up ideas to increase market share when one of the managers said she had read about a store on the East Coast that had hosted an event for singles to meet each other," Williams says. "We decided to give it a try."

The event was leaked to Seattle newspapers and television stations, which gave it plenty of news space and air time. A local radio station showed up to provide listeners with a live broadcast, reporting that it was "standing room only." There were so many people in attendance at the following year's "Singles Night" that the fire department closed the doors out of overcapacity concerns. "I know of at least one married couple that fell in love at 'Singles Night,'" says Weymer.

SHARING OUR STORIES

Synchronized Shoppers Become Parade Event Favorite

From Hawaiian Days to Singles Nights, the company's stores in the mid-1990s were an incubator of performance art talent. Yet, few shows to come out of the employee brain trust compare with the famed grocery cart drill teams. Poulsbo Market Place gets credit for developing the first drill team, in which several employees pushed grocery carts in front of them in unison, marching to music much like a well-trained squad of soldiers. The success of the Poulsbo squad spawned teams at other stores, which sometimes marched in the same parade.

The Bainbridge Town & Country's team was a serious group of marchers. "There were about thirty of us, and we would regularly meet and practice at our store and at the Poulsbo store, because they had more space there," says Susan Calhoun. "We marched in the annual Fourth of July parade in Bainbridge in the 1990s, which always started at the library at one o'clock and then came down Madison and turned to go down Main Street."

The Bainbridge team marched to a live band that rode in the back of a pickup truck and played Dolly Parton's song "Nine to Five" from the movie by the same name. "We dressed in pants with matching shirts and ball caps and had these egg cartons with ribbons on them to look like batons," says Susan. "We'd weave in and out of the cars in perfect, OK, near-perfect formation, and then come together and do a kick line. When we hit Winslow Green, it was such a tremendous rush. There was this sea of people, and everyone was screaming because we were such public figures, working in the store and all. It was so much fun. For a girl who grew up on a farm in the Midwest, the connection with the community this company gave me made me feel like I belonged, right from the beginning."

Ballard Market also hosted a "Cruz Nite" celebration of the music and clothing styles of the 1950s. It became the first Town & Country store in Seattle to sponsor a precision drill cart team—a group of employees that marched in unison, each pushing a shopping cart in front of him or her. "Ballard stood for fun and creativity," says Larry Nakata. "It was ahead of its time, and the staff had some great ideas."

The idea for the drill cart team, however, originated with Poulsbo Market Place, which famously marched to Dolly Parton's song "Nine to Five" at Viking Fest parades. On occasion, members of the team would square off in a drill competition.

8:31 AM

TOWN & COUNTRY

Store director Rick Pedersen discusses upcoming merchandising efforts with department managers (left to right) Tracey Beck, Don Thornton, Sharen Iversen, Bryan Biggs, and Vern Nakata at T&C's weekly MAP meeting.

MAP Meeting
March 14, 2007

A Passion for Food & Fun

AGENDA

- MAP REVIEW –
- BIG BOARD REVIEW
- BRIDGE CLOSURE – HOW'S IT GOING?
- RETAIL EXPERIENCE DIALOGUE / ROUNDTABLE / KAIZEN / THE TAO JONES – PICK ONE EACH WEEK.
- MERCHANDISING
  - APRIL / MAY CALENDAR - FINAL
  - HALIBUT – MAR 12
  - CAKEWALK – MAR 22 TO 27
  - ARTICHOKES – MAR 27
  - PEANUTS AND POPCORN – MAR 30 TO APR 2
  - EARTH DAY 2007
- 50TH ANNIVERSARY PLANNING

With Greg Johnson and Bill Weymer, Don Nakata launched a new, automated planning and forecasting strategy at Ballard Market called MAP, for Management Action Planning. MAP later was introduced to other company stores and remains a guiding principle today. Left: An early MAP session in Ballard.

MAPPING THE FUTURE

Leveraging Greg Johnson's technological skill and Bill Weymer's business talents, Don launched a new planning and forecasting strategy at Ballard Market called MAP, for Management Action Planning. MAP drew inspiration from the company's Product Awareness through Demonstration, or PAD, program, in which department managers came together to share their experiences. MAP took PAD several steps forward in terms of collaboration. Department managers used the automated system to create forecasts for a coming quarter, projecting their sales, profits, and labor costs. These metrics were then measured against actual quarterly performance. After a successful implementation, MAP was rolled out to the other stores.

In 1987, Don and Bill, through the EFM subsidiary, opened another store on Northeast 20th Street in Bellevue, a posh suburb east of Seattle. Although the store, Overlake Market, was next to an interstate highway and had been extensively remodeled, it was in the back of a shopping center and remained relatively hidden from view. Three years hence, the company sold Overlake Market and set aside this capital for future investments.

Mo Nakata passed away in 1985 and was remembered at his funeral for his boundless enthusiasm and bravery during World War II. His buoyant personality had lifted many spirits on the island, and the funeral attendees filled Eagle Harbor Congregational Church's pews. "I once had a half-hour meeting with Mo at his house, and I remember sitting there thinking, 'I hope this goes on the rest of the afternoon,'" says Art Jones, former AG president. "That's how wonderful he was." Mo's shares in the company were passed on to his sons, Larry and Ron.

His lifelong friend gone, Ed Loverich officially retired, though he loved few things more than visiting T&C and schmoozing with former colleagues and longtime customers. Big Ed sold his shares back to the company, so he and Billie could comfortably enjoy the rest of their lives at their waterfront home, which overlooked the ferries making their daily treks to and from Seattle. Their sister-in-law Elaine Loverich also retired, and her bookkeeping duties at T&C were taken over by Wayne Loverich's wife, Mari.

With Don leading the company, its destiny was in good hands. Don was now completely in charge of Town & Country Market, Inc. "Don was the essence of quiet leadership," says Bill Weymer, "an amazing person whose personality left an imprint on everyone he met. His leadership style was collaborative and inspiring. Like Socrates, he wouldn't tell you what to do; he'd ask questions so you knew instinctively what to do."

WELL-EARNED RECOGNITION

The supermarket industry recognized the extraordinary leader it had in Don Nakata. In 1988, *Food Dealer* magazine, published by the Washington State Food Dealers Association, named Don Grocer of the Year at their eighty-ninth annual convention. In his keynote speech, Morrie Olson of Olson's Foods said of Don, "Service is important to this man, and his insistence on good customer service is evident in each of his stores."

In an article profiling Don, *Food Dealer* magazine stated that he "makes sure his employees play an important part in the operations of the stores, drawing on the staff to be participative in management, and soliciting ideas for the promotions that keep his stores so much in the newspapers."

Don accepted the award at the podium accompanied by Ellen. Characteristically, he gave full credit to his employees: "I am just part of that team," he said. He also spoke about his own "personal heroes"—the founders of Town & Country Market, Inc.—and emphasized the important role played by his father in his life and work. "It was an emotional moment for me," recalls Larry Nakata, whose late father, Mo, was still very much on his mind. "Don's message was clear: we were here not only because of our own efforts, but because of the efforts of those who came before us."

At the dawn of the 1990s, the company's four stores were at the forefront of modern, trend-setting grocery retailing, prompting *Progressive Grocer* magazine, a national trade publication, to name it to the prestigious Honor Roll of America's "Outstanding Independent Grocers" in 1989. Yet Don was touched most deeply by an etched glass painting of the Poulsbo store that employees gave him the same year. On it were carved four words he had coined to inspire them—Achieve, Believe, Conceive, and Desire.

Despite these various tributes and accolades, the period was a challenging one for Town & Country Market, Inc., as competitors planted flags throughout its regional base. On Bainbridge Island, the situation was acute: Safeway had decided to build a supermarket on the site of the old Village Foods. The company's flagship store was vulnerable for the first time. In the spirit of "quiet confidence," Don took a deep breath and braced for the impact.

At the culmination of the Washington State Food Dealers Association convention in 1988, Don Nakata, above, was named Grocer of the Year, an honor he shared with the many employees and coworkers who over the years had helped him shape the company into a modern, trend-setting grocery retailer. Accompanying him at the podium to accept the award was his wife, Ellen, and in the audience an emotional crowd of T&C employees had gathered to cheer on their leader.

CHAPTER FOUR

A Destination in Sight

The day in 1990 that Safeway opened on Bainbridge Island, Town & Country experienced a drop in customer traffic. Although remodeling of the store was under way to differentiate T&C from the retail giant, the quietude was unsettling. "Don and I were in the office and saw a group of Winslow merchants coming toward the store carrying helium balloons. They brought them in and placed them near the checkout stands, signifying their support for our store," says bookkeeper Mari Loverich. "We broke down."

Patience and perseverance—the quintessence of *gaman*—were the store's saving grace. The renovations were not rushed and, in fact, would not be finished until months after the Safeway opening. Among the changes were a full-service deli with home-cooked food and a salad bar with natural greens. "We wanted customers to be able to buy restaurant-style food and not just the usual supermarket fare," says Wayne Loverich.

A new food service team also was on tap. Wayne Loverich had hired a former restaurateur from New York City, Joel Levy, to conduct product demonstrations as a member of this team. "Gary Reese, my grocery manager at the time, came to my office and said, 'Wayne, I have a guy downstairs demonstrating his product, Hometown #1 Seasoning. You need to see this demonstration.'"

Wayne watched transfixed for about half an hour. Joel had a crowd of customers around him, everyone bantering back and forth about food while laughing, eating, and buying a lot of Hometown #1 Seasoning. "We were looking for someone who knew food and could demonstrate and educate our customers about the many specialty foods we carried," Wayne says.

Joel fit the bill. A New Yorker and a self-described "foodie," Joel had worked with Time/Life Books' cookbook division, where he came in contact with cookbook writer, teacher, and consultant Michael Field, who focused on the principles of classic cooking. Through the years, Joel had amassed an encyclopedic knowledge of gourmet food that he parlayed into a series of successful Manhattan restaurants. "I had a long conversation with Joel about our plans as we walked the store and looked at products," Wayne recalls. "After much conversation about our vision and goals, Joel was retained as a consultant, demonstrator, and educator for the store. He fit right in as customers and staff enjoyed his personal interaction and the tasty foods he promoted and talked about."

Joel subsequently helped design T&C's deli and demonstration table, and recommended using stainless steel for its meat display cases—today the norm in all company stores. "With Joel's assistance, our deli staff produced 'We Make It Here' products that were many steps above normal supermarket deli food in taste," Wayne adds. "This deli was the beginning of all future delis in our company."

As the modern era dawned, Don Nakata put his energies and talents to devising a supermarket that would draw in crowds from all over the region. Central Market, opposite, was the culmination of everything he had envisioned, a place where people could buy the freshest produce, meat, and seafood while perusing food demos, special promotions and events, and delicious deli samples. Right: One of many copper sculptures by Bainbridge Island artist Michele Van Slyke displayed throughout the Shoreline Central Market store.

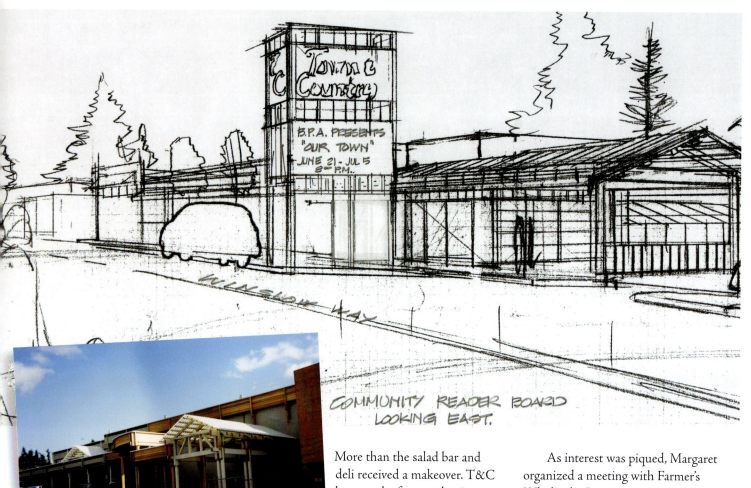

Community Reader Board Looking East.

To accommodate the growing deli and wine cellar as well as the changing tastes of the people of Bainbridge, T&C contracted local architect Miles Yanick to redesign the aging store. Top: A conceptual drawing by Dale Cox shows the newly redesigned store front, which brought the espresso bar and expanding floral department out from under tents and integrated them into the store. Above: T&C under renovation.

More than the salad bar and deli received a makeover. T&C became the first market in Washington state to provide a substantial array of organic fruits and vegetables. Credit goes to Margaret Clark, a produce clerk hired at the store in 1986. Margaret grew organic produce in her garden and was on a first-name basis with area organic farmers. To satisfy the desires of a few customers, she ordered organic produce from the farmers. "It caught on, and the produce manager said I could start labeling items that were organic," she says.

As interest was piqued, Margaret organized a meeting with Farmer's Wholesale Cooperative, an organization representing organic growers, to provide a steady supply of their produce to the store. She encouraged local farmers like Brian McWhorter, John Gunning, Dennis and Bonnie White, Gerry Malko, Omrao Bagwandin, and others to grow organic produce and helped a few of them devise packaging and marketing strategies. In preparation for the 1989 store remodel, Margaret wrote up a business plan for organic produce as a separate store department to assure needed staffing, training, and space. Don gave the plan his approval, and when T&C reopened, customers were introduced to the Organic and Specialty Produce Department. "We did very well, and I got a bit famous for awhile," Margaret laughs.

She is being humble. Associated Grocers asked her to present a seminar on organic produce to its retail members, prompting the Food Marketing Institute to invite her to speak at their annual convention in Chicago. Margaret's name soon was a fixture in produce trade magazines. She became the chair of the Washington State Department of Agriculture's Organic Certification Board and, in 1991, joined the United States Department of Agriculture as the first retail representative on its National Organic Standards Board.

NEW DEPARTMENTS

The renovation also provided larger quarters for fresh meats and seafood. To carve out the new space required, an addition to the original building was constructed over the parking lot, preserving needed parking spaces. The basement was remodeled to include distinctive, stand-alone departments, an expansive wine cellar, a housewares shop, and a natural and bulk foods department. Customers had the choice of checkout stands on either floor. What didn't change was the service. "Customers felt a connection to employees, as if they all were part of one big family," says Rolly Radwick, the company's insurance agent.

Safeway pared T&C's customer base for a few weeks, as people visited it out of curiosity. Ultimately, the newcomer had little impact and T&C retained its position as the community's emotional core. This was particularly evident during the Great Blizzard of 1990, which mowed down trees, felling power lines and leaving many without electricity for a week. The store also lost power and the outside tents were destroyed, but it stayed open. "People came in with their horror stories, needing to tell someone what they'd been

---

SHARING OUR STORIES

Island Residents Find Warm Welcome, Hot Coffee During Blackouts

The Great Blizzard of 1990 was not the only time Bainbridge islanders found themselves without power. In fact, two or three power outages a winter are common, with at least one lasting more than a day. "In the scheme of things, they're quite frequent here," says Wayne Loverich.

Since the majority of islanders lack generators and T&C has one, it is common, in fact routine, for a good portion of Bainbridge's population to make their way past felled power lines and down snowy embankments to the store. "They come here for something to eat and for someone to share their stories with—whether we have power or not," Loverich says.

The store installed the generator in the late 1970s, although the electricity it provides is scant. "We use it to keep a string of lights going along the aisles and to run the cash registers at the front end," says Wayne. "It doesn't keep the refrigerators going. Instead, we open the front and back doors to let in the cold and then open the refrigerator doors. Typically the food survives, depending how long the outage lasts."

On such days when the islanders seek shelter at T&C, they are provided free coffee, cookies, and water while supplies last. Customers appreciate having a place to go to when times are tough. In a survey of what shoppers like best about T&C, one responded, "I want to thank [the store] for going the extra mile when we need it most—for remaining open during storms and power outages—and for providing that warm cup of coffee, a place to gather, and nourishment in every sense of the word."

Wayne says the tradition will not end. When the snows come next year and the power blinks off, "as soon as their driveways permit, they make their way here."

10:25 AM

BALLARD MARKET

Produce clerk Dan Sheehan stocks organic apples. With a small footprint but high sales volume, the produce department at Ballard Market requires almost constant restocking—making its produce some of the freshest in the Seattle area.

Margaret Clark, right, whose motto is "local plus proper post-harvest handling equals fresh," is credited with T&C's commitment to organic foods by heeding customers' early interests, studying and practicing organic farming, and launching the now company-wide organic produce division.

through," says Margaret Clark. "We tried to have something warm for them to drink and made lots of soups. Candles and flashlights illuminated the aisles. Here was where islanders felt sympathy and kinship."

EXPANDING THE VISION

As the Bainbridge store expanded its facilities and offerings, Don hunted for a location to open another store. The EFM subsidiary subsequently was folded into Town & Country Market, Inc., and along with Wayne Loverich and Greg Johnson, Bill Weymer was provided shares in the corporation. The new store was the former Larry's Market located north of Seattle in the city of Shoreline, Washington's fifteenth largest city. The store's surrounding area along Aurora Avenue had fallen on hard times and consisted of many used car dealerships, fast food restaurants, and older shopping centers. Don was undisturbed by the dinginess of the shopping center supporting the store and the market's small size, only 29,000 square feet. As with Ballard Market, he could see potential where others did not. "We leased the store with the idea that we could acquire the Pay 'N Save drugstore next door, but they were unwilling to let go," Weymer says.

The new store opened in September 1990 as Shoreline Price Chopper, a discount format aimed at suiting the recessionary economy. Ron Nakata set up a larger produce department, while other departments received minor face-lifts. The store struggled, however, as competition from larger stores and its small size proved formidable obstacles. Although T&C had experience running a discount operation in the 1970s (Viking Mark-It Foods), expectations had changed. Poulsbo had upscaled to meet the needs of its evolving market, and the company realized it could never be considered the low-price leader in a competitive market such as Seattle. The themes "Know who you are" and "Be true to yourself" proved their relevancy.

In 1991, another new store joined the company in Greenwood—like Ballard, a suburb of Seattle with a very strong identity. The store had previously been a California-owned Lucky's and subsequently operated as an independently owned Hayden's store, a Bellingham-based grocer and good friend of Town & Country. Don had passed on leasing it in the mid-1980s while the company was developing the Ballard

SHARING OUR STORIES

Suppliers Share Town & Country's Passion for High Quality

Town & Country has long sought to partner with vendors and suppliers who share its commitment to high quality and responsible business practices. One of the earliest such partnerships was formed with commercial fisherman Bruce Gore, whose operations are based on Bainbridge Island. Bruce had developed frozen-at-sea techniques that resulted in articles in the *New York Times* and *Washington Post* as well as praise from Julia Child.

The articles caught the attention of Don Nakata in 1982. "Back then retail stores couldn't get the highest quality fish," Bruce says. "Don called me and we met. I recognized immediately that he and I were spiritually connected. He had the same philosophical regard for food that I

have. Salmon is the physical embodiment and the essence of the people of the Northwest, a wonderful gift from nature. It needs to be treated and handled with the greatest reverence to protect its intrinsic value. Don had the same view. We became instant friends and business partners."

Bruce educated store employees about his own fishing methods and handling techniques, giving slide shows to inspire them to treat his catch the same way he did—with the utmost care. "When T&C started retailing our fish in the 1980s, they were selling the highest quality, sashimi grade salmon in the world," Bruce says. "No other store had fish of this quality."

Bulk coffee supplier Equal Exchange has also arranged for meetings with store staff, but its visitors come from over three thousand miles away.

"We had the first woman farmer ever to visit the U.S. as part of a Fair Trade delegation come to the store on Bainbridge," recalls Tom Hanlon-Wilde, western sales manager for the fair trade organization that supplies T&C's six markets. "She enjoyed every minute of her trip, as everyone was so nice to her. Since then T&C has brought in another three farmers from some of the other cooperatives we work with. We're learning so much working with these people."

Tom came to the attention of Wayne Loverich in 1997. "I was at the store and Wayne and I discussed the idea of bulk coffee provided by farmers in Omtepe, an island in Lake Nicaragua, which is a sort of sister city to Bainbridge," Tom recalls. "We started on a small scale with about four feet of display space, and it just grew over the years."

But no vendor relationship is more of a partnership than that between T&C and organic farmer Brian McWhorter. In 1985 he ventured into T&C on Bainbridge Island to shop for groceries when he ran into Margaret Clark, who worked in the produce department. "I was one of the first organic farmers in the area and Margaret was in the process of developing the store's organic produce department," Brian recalls. "She became very excited about my supplying the store. She was so dedicated to organic produce, as were the Nakatas, who supported all her efforts in this regard."

Today, he grows a wide variety of produce for the stores on roughly twenty acres, most of them leased. One of the locations is the old strawberry farm that Jitsuzo Nakata purchased on the corner of Wyatt Way and Weaver Avenue in 1924. "We farmed about three of the farm's thirteen acres last year, growing zucchini, cucumbers, beans, corn, squash, and sunflowers—all certified organic," Brian says. "The Nakatas are trying to keep things local to provide the absolute freshest produce."

A large portrait of Brian, along with photographs of other local and regional farmers the company does business with, hangs in the Town & Country Market's produce department, a testament to the importance of these farmers. Next year Brian hopes to grow another organic fruit on the old Nakata farm—strawberries. "It just might come back," he says.

"Pure bliss is when you arrive at that brief moment when everything is set out perfectly and no one has touched it yet," Ballard Market produce manager Joe Pulicicchio says. "Yet, while it may look like art, our chief objective is to sell excellent produce—the best anywhere.

The Price Chopper format for the company's new supermarket in Greenwood, below, in 1991 was an attempt to lure shoppers seeking to conserve their food and grocery expenses. Despite its small size and nearby competitors, the store's scrappy nature struck a chord with the diverse community.

store, believing the organization could only handle one new store at a time. It was a good decision: the Hayden group eventually shuttered the market, leaving it vacant for months. "AG offered us a very favorable lease, and we took it," says Larry Nakata.

Following a major cleanup and upgrades to the perishable departments, the store reopened as Greenwood Price Chopper. At 19,000 square feet, it was small, yet its scrappiness was its appeal. The neighborhood made it their own, much in the way Ballard Market had captured that community's pride and spirit. Clever promotions like the "15 Hour Meat Sale" hit the target, but the store's abiding success was its staff. They knew customers by name and assisted diverse community organizations, from local schools and churches to Little League baseball teams.

Town & Country Market, Inc. opened a corporate office in Ballard in 1991, where new controller Cindy Schneider worked the numbers. Cindy previously had been employed by a local accounting firm that audited the company's tax returns and other financial records. She worked closely with Larry Nakata, who had become the company's finance officer in addition to running the Poulsbo store, and with Greg Johnson, at the forefront of developing automated forecasting and budgeting systems. The latter abetted Cindy's gradual internalization of financial information. "Don was a big-picture person and not particularly detail-oriented, and he leaned on the rest of us for financial data," Cindy says.

A PRODUCE PICASSO

The Ballard store's phenomenal success continued. Fresh, high-quality produce remained a differentiating strength, and the addition of Bob Sherry, formerly of Associated Grocers, cemented this category as an area of focused dedication. The produce team was further strengthened with the hiring in 1987 of a new produce manager named Joe Pulicicchio, who'd cut his teeth managing produce at Mega Foods in Tacoma.

With these changes in place, Ron Nakata transferred back to Poulsbo to assist produce operations there and eventually expanded his responsibilities to include moving between Seattle and Poulsbo to help out where most needed.

"A wholesaler said to me, 'You just have to work for the Nakatas. They're the best people on the planet,'" Joe says. He commuted nearly fifty miles each morning to his job as Ballard Market's produce manager, a job he loved. "Produce is the last great commodity that is still exciting," says Joe. "It's susceptible to supply and demand swings and is affected by the weather, soil conditions, and sunshine. If you don't move it, it rots, and every season it's a bit better or a bit worse."

He searched the marketplace for top-notch produce to differentiate Ballard Market. When a particularly great batch of California strawberries came on the market, Joe did not shy away from buying a full load of ten pallets. "I knew our customers had to have them," he explains. He priced them at $3 a flat, when competitors sold lesser-quality strawberries at $7.98 a flat. "It was Easter, and we sold them all—more than one thousand flats," he recalls.

Displaying fresh produce is an art form in Joe's hands. He exhibits different fruits and vegetables according to their colors, painting an Impressionist landscape. "Pure bliss is when you arrive at that brief moment when everything is set out perfectly and no one has touched it yet," he says. "Yet, while it may look like art, our chief objective is to sell excellent produce—the best anywhere. That doesn't mean there aren't values. A peach that tastes like a million bucks isn't going to sell for twenty dollars. We try to strike a balance between perfection and price."

Poulsbo Market Place also solidified its standing during the decade. Each week the store published the *Poulsbo Market Place Newsletter* apprising employees of birth announcements, 401(k) plan meetings, and helpful information like the earth-friendly uses of vinegar as a cleaning substitute. When Larry's lung collapsed in 1993, he thanked all who sent flowers, writing in the newsletter, "The doctors said a lung collapse usually occurs in people who are 'young, tall, and thin.' Well, one out of three isn't too bad."

Employees called their store PMP. They loved their jobs and customers loved them. Many wrote about their experiences, which were printed in the newsletter. "I drive from Bremerton once a week to shop at Poulsbo Market Place, bypassing other grocery stores along the way," a letter from 1994 states. "The journey is worth it. There are things that motivate me to shop at the market—organic produce, the best selection of bulk dried goods I've seen anywhere, and environmentally sound paper and cleaning products. Shopping, which is usually a chore, has been an hour of delightful discovery every week."

The store and its employees sponsored a great number of charitable and philanthropic endeavors, such as "Shop for a Cure," in which local celebrities like Russell Johnson, "the Professor" on the *Gilligan's Island* TV

Larry Nakata, top, was the longtime store director at Poulsbo Market Place. Larry had graduated from the University of Washington with a degree in business and, like his cousin Don, served in the armed forces, in Larry's case as a stenographer with the U.S. Army. Above: An electric blue jacket worn and much loved by the employees.

12:22 PM

INFORMATION SYSTEMS

IS team members (from left) Tim Clifford, Mike Brooks, Craig McKeel, and Scott Weaver discuss updates to the corporate Web site. The IS department, housed at "The Villa" in the small Kitsap Peninsula community of Kingston, maintains all information technology for the company, from checkout scanners to ordering systems, and keeps a complete working scanner and cash register on a desk for testing and programming purposes.

series, bagged groceries, with a percentage of sales going to the American Cancer Society. Johnson lives on Bainbridge Island with his wife. On another occasion, the Seattle Mariners baseball team sent over a then-unknown player named Edgar Martinez to sign baseballs. The longtime Mariner—he spent his entire career with the team—nowadays is recognized as the greatest designated hitter in the history of the sport.

Susan Allen, Don and Ellen's daughter, returned to the family business in 1993. The following year, Larry was named "Person of the Year" by the Poulsbo Chamber of Commerce. The longtime store director accepted the award on behalf of employees, "in recognition of the fine job that you are doing now and have done over the years for our community," he stated. "You're making a real difference. I've known that for a long time, and it's nice to be reminded that others, too, are aware of your contribution."

A CENTRAL TENET

The year 1994 marks an important juncture in the history of Town & Country Market, Inc. For some time, Don had mulled the idea of a "destination store" drawing in shoppers from beyond the core geographic area. The store would blend fun, excitement, and entertainment with high-quality produce, seafood, meats, and delicious prepared meals to create an adventure in shopping. He expressed his idea at a meeting of store directors and other key personnel. The attendees had just reported challenging financial news, and Don's introduction of the concept seemed out of place. "Had anyone else been apprised of our

numbers, their immediate reaction would be, 'Batten down the hatches and start trimming,'" says Greg Johnson, who was in attendance.

Don didn't blink, however. "He never let numbers dictate a change in the company's growth strategy or his own values and philosophy," says Greg. "Instead, he announced that we would scale up to build the destination store. He then emphatically stated his confidence in us. We left the meeting energized."

Instrumental in conceptualizing the destination store was DW Green, president and CEO of DW Green Company, an advertising agency from whom Don occasionally had sought advertising assistance. Over the course of nine months, Don and Green met several times to exchange ideas. Green said he and his associate Ron Short had come across a grocery store in Texas named "Central Market."

"I'd always liked the sound of it and told Don and the T&C team during a planning meeting that it would make a great name for a store," says Green. "The word 'central' denoted a destination, and it fit Poulsbo, which was in the center of Kitsap County. Don and the T&C team liked the name and it stuck." For the last six months before Central Market opened, a team from Town & Country Market, Inc. would head to Green's Tacoma office each Friday to review the concept and vision behind the store—analyzing each department in depth.

Central Market, advertised as Kitsap County's "first destination food store," was a concept developed by Don Nakata and marketing consultant DW Green. Dale Cox's conceptual drawing of Miles Yanick's plan for the Poulsbo Central Market, left, demonstrates the clean, modern lines and amenities the store evinced. The overriding principle Don and Green adhered to was that shopping didn't have to be a chore; in fact, it could be an enjoyable experience. Below: A tractor and corn stalks decorate the newly built Poulsbo Central Market.

MORE THAN A MARKET

More profoundly, Green and Don and the T&C team developed a revolutionary plan to attract people with low-cost fresh produce, meats, and seafood. In the grocery industry, these items customarily are high-margin products and not competitively priced. "Don wanted produce to drive the price perception, and the best produce at that," Green says. "Fortunately, he had Joe Pulicicchio in his corner." Joe had graduated to become the produce specialist for all company stores.

Associated Grocers gave a presentation to Don, Larry, and other senior managers about the kind of store AG wanted the company to build. "It was basically a copy of the Food Pavilion that was in Silverdale and other areas," Larry says. "We felt this was not a strong enough format to do the things that we desired. We felt that we had to do something very unique and powerful to draw customers from long distances."

Emerging technologies played a role in these deliberations. CAD (computer-aided design) systems had been developed that permitted collaborative design electronically. Greg purchased an inexpensive CAD system and programmed the footprint of the planned store into it. He drew some plans into the footprint and then faxed them to Don, who added his own tweaks,

"Not only was this the first green commercial building in the county and the state, it was pretty much the first in the nation for a building of its size and scale," says Dave Peters, Kitsap County Solid Waste Division's recycling coordinator. "It ended up being a textbook example of how to put together a green building."

allocating more space for this department and less space for that one. The board also provided their input. Back and forth the designs went until they were finalized in the CAD system. Once a basic configuration was achieved, the design went to the department heads, specialists, industry experts, and several employees. "We solicited input from a lot of people," says Greg. "These ideas were captured in the CAD system and then given to AG. The real beauty of the process was how rapidly we could communicate and involve many brilliant minds into creating a store unlike anything in the area. Indeed, hundreds of people can be credited for the store's design."

Central Market opened in Poulsbo on August 23, 1995, marking a major new direction for the company. At 69,000 square feet, it was the largest store in the corporate pantheon by far and the area's first destination store. The modern-looking building was designed by architect Miles Yanick on land leased to Associated Grocers from Hattaland Partners (Town & Country is the subtenant). Hattaland's general partner Sam Clarke, a Nakata family friend, approached Don and Larry about the prospect of building their planned destination store at the site, even though Fred Meyer, a regional chain, had previously signed a letter of intent. "Sam said, 'We've known you guys for a long time and think you should have first crack at this location,'" Larry says. "Looking back, it was a gift based on a personal friendship that blossomed into a great business relationship."

GOING GREEN

Great attention was given to the perishable produce, meat, seafood, and natural foods departments, which were larger and more open to public interactions. Other features also were novel. "We had planned to put a video rental facility up front, but at the last minute changed it to a pizza and hot dog stand," says Susan Allen. "It was a big market and we figured people might want something to eat. If it felt right, my father could shift gears immediately."

As project manager, Larry had been approached by the Kitsap County Solid Waste Division with a proposal to make the market the first in Washington state to be built out of recycled materials. "We'd won a grant to promote a 'green' commercial building in the county and had heard that Larry was planning a new store," says Dave Peters, the division's recycling coordinator. "I met with Larry and explained our interest in the store's being our demonstration project. He sat there, listened, and then put his head into his hands. I figured he was politely trying to tell me to go away. Instead, he looked up and said, 'This fits our mission to be responsible stewards of the environment.'"

Much of the store's structure is recycled content, including floor mats made with recycled tire rubber, parking stops made with recycled milk jugs, and steel studs and roof decking made of recycled steel. The store's concrete floor was finished with a sealer that improved its appearance and allowed its washing with water alone, thereby eliminating the use of toxic floor cleaners and finishers. The building's surfaces also were painted with low volatile organic compound (VOC) paints. "Not only was this the first green commercial building in the county and the state, it was pretty much the first in the nation for a building of its size and scale," Peters says. "It ended up being a textbook example of how to put together a green building."

When the Solid Waste Division later met with the state's home builders association, the executive director asked Peters how to make a green building. "I told him to drive to Central Market," he says. The store was a forerunner for the National Home Builders Association's "Built Green" program of today.

Central Market integrated other environmental initiatives. The building is sheltered partially by the earth, built into a hill on the site to make it less invasive to the surroundings, while also providing heating and cooling benefits via the hill's natural insulation. To preserve the natural wetlands located on the site, Sam Clarke and his partners, the local owners of the property, mitigated six wetlands at the site and built a single, higher quality, double capacity wetland across the street. Eventually, Hattaland Partners conveyed the wetland pond to the city, and the pond today is an integral part of a passive park. The company also elected to use a new environmentally responsible refrigerant gas, 404A, to refrigerate its hundreds of medium- and low-temperature cases.

ONE TOWN, TWO MARKETS

The twenty-four-hour Central Market posed obvious competition for Poulsbo Market Place. Initial plans called for closing the older store once the new one opened, but the company still had nine years left on the lease and the rent was low. Don and Larry also were concerned about the competitive impact of putting the site on the market. Yet, it was customer

In 1995, Central Market, above, was unique for the times. The building embraced many "green" initiatives that today are more common, or at least more talked about. For many years, it was the model for a sustainable commercial building, a bona fide "Green Grocery," as the newspaper article, right, suggests.

The staff at Poulsbo Central Market put their creative energies in overdrive, coming up with innovative ways to make shopping a more enjoyable experience. From the sweetest corn harvested hours before its delivery, above, to the inimitable Farmer Jo, a.k.a. meat cutter Bryan Johansen, left, bedecked in his traditional costume for informative tours, Central Market was an entertaining winner.

loyalty that tipped the scales. "Many older customers said they'd never shop at another store since they liked the original one so much," says Larry. "We kept it open to see what would happen."

Poulsbo Market Place retained the bulk of its business, while Central Market left the gates slowly. "The store had hit its 'J-Curve,'" says Larry.

The "J-Curve" refers to sliding business volume that hits a low point and then turns up. Even though the Central Market concept was untested and the cash outlay for the new store was huge, Don took the downward trend in stride. "My dad had great confidence in the store, which was the culmination of everything he believed in," says Susan Allen. "He knew that people eventually would love the store as much as he did, and that it was the right thing to do. He was a very patient man."

Central Market rebounded, becoming what Don had envisioned—a destination store. Customers from an ever-widening radius didn't let the driving distance dissuade them. "People came here the first time just to see the store," says checker Debbie Tuson. "Then they brought their friends from out of town to see it, and then their friends brought their friends."

The store also became famous for its events and promotions. Don had decided to terminate weekly newspaper advertising for Central Market (and later at other stores), diverting the funding to unique customer experiences. "We'd do things like bring in a local corn farmer who'd harvested his crop hours before," says store director Tom Hall. "He'd park his truck outside and sell twenty ears for a dollar. We called it the 'Corn Festival' and it became an annual event. One year a woman bought thirty ears; the next year she came back and bought eight hundred ears for her neighborhood block party. Another time this fellow showed up in a Volkswagen Beetle and said, 'Fill it with as much corn as you can.' He didn't mean just the trunk."

Then there was Farmer Jo. Bryan Johansen, a meat cutter at the market, regularly donned bib overalls and a straw hat to become the store's unofficial ambassador for the kid set. "As Farmer Jo, Bryan taught the kids about food safety, organic produce, and the food pyramid," Hall says. "He had a tractor outside with a hay wagon hitched to it that he drove the kids in. The kids and their parents, whose time was freed to shop in peace, loved it."

"Don believed if people had a great experience, they would come back again and again," says CPA Steve Finley. DW Green chimes in, "If there was a Nobel Prize for grocery retailing, Town & Country would win it."

Town & Country Market, Inc. also endured challenging conditions at the Shoreline store. "We went from the Price Chopper format to the Thriftway format, and it still didn't do well," says Cindy Schneider. "For a long time, it just wasn't a winner."

For Don, these varied trials were compounded by personal pressures. In 1995, his beloved father, John, passed away. John had led the Nakatas into the grocery business as Charley Bremer's apprentice at the Eagle Harbor Market. He had saved his money to buy the store, tearing down the old barbershop and family home to build a new Eagle Harbor Market only to lose it to the inequities of the war. F. Scott Fitzgerald wrote that "there are no second acts in American lives," but John had proved him wrong,

SHARING OUR STORIES

Central Market Lures Customer with Creative Concepts, Seasonal Fare

From "Corn Festivals" with local farmers hawking a field's worth of corn to genial "Farmer Jo," Central Market in Poulsbo, which avoids advertising in favor of customer word of mouth, can be a pretty jumpin' jivin' place on a gray, rainy day.

It is not uncommon for fishermen just a few hours off their boats to show up with their catch—Kitsap County's version of Seattle's Pike Place Market. "We'll have two hundred pounds of halibut in the front lobby area on ice, with our cutters custom-filleting the fish for shoppers," says store director Tom Hall. "We call it 'Dock to Door in 24,' although the fish arrives here in much less than a day."

Hall says his staff's creative concepts "often come while walking through the store and closing our eyes, which somehow helps you think outside the box. One time we had this idea to put telephones in the aisles so kids could come in, and if they didn't have enough money to pay for a local phone call, they could call their homes. Also, if Dad forgot the shopping list or was confused about what item to get, he could call home to Mom. Our thinking was that this would be a way to connect with the community."

The "close your eyes" concept was borrowed from Don Nakata. "At meetings to define the store, Don would ask us to close our eyes and imagine reasons why Mrs. Smith and her kids would drive all the way from Sequim to the store," Hall says. "We imagined things like big, expansive 'fresh' departments like produce and events that would make the store entertaining for parents and kids. We still do it."

11:30 AM

POULSBO CENTRAL MARKET

Friends Carolyn Flack, Julie Donegan, and Victoria Wilson catch up while Mealtime Express chef Michael Jackson cooks up burgers and hot sandwiches for a lunchtime crowd. Lunchtime is one of the busiest times of day at the Poulsbo market, when its prepared foods draw workers and students from nearby businesses and schools.

In 1995, John Nakata passed away, leaving his wife, Pauline (center) and their sons (clockwise from left of Pauline) Wayne, Vern, Don, and Bob. John's brother Mo had died a decade earlier, and his partner Ed passed away in 1996. The next generation banded together to make sure the company not only stayed strong but also stayed true to the founders' vision.

repurchasing Eagle Harbor Market, and capitalizing T&C with Mo and Ed.

The following year, Ed, too, passed on. He had thrilled islanders with his one-handed basketball shot and entertained them as a seven-foot-tall Hawaiian King. During his last few years, Big Ed suffered from Alzheimer's disease, and his many visits to the store helped ground his memories. Newspapers around the state carried news of his death. "Here's to 'Ashcan' Loverich," the headline in the *Bainbridge Island Review* toasted. "He was the Legendary Basketball Trailblazer. And the Giant Giant. And don't forget the King of Customer Service. Many can feel that they were his best friend." Don's three "personal heroes," as he always called the founders, were gone.

The troubling financial numbers didn't intrude on Don's big-picture thinking, and he looked toward the future with his customary vigor, planning and strategizing with top lieutenants other ingenious ways to enhance customer experiences. He hired Mike Latham, a former Tandy Corp. executive with an interest in food safety, to inculcate food safety practices throughout the stores. Mike became a certified food inspector and unveiled a formal food safety program that improved food preparation and provided safer products to customers. He also successfully lobbied the Washington State Liquor Control Board to allow the company's stores to perform in-house liquor audits. "We were the first to do this, and we've been 100 percent compliant ever since," Mike says.

GUIDED BY GAMAN

Don always was fine-tuning the company's philosophy and mission. A perpetual student of business theories, he latched onto three Japanese concepts in 1997 to help guide employees in their work lives. One, *gaman* (patience and perseverance), was evident in Don's own approach to business. The others included *kaizen*, which means continuous improvement, and *umami*, which means peak of perfection. Don wove these themes into the fabric of the company and employees embraced it. "In American culture we measure success in home runs, whereas Japanese companies measure success by hitting singles every day," says Greg Johnson.

The company's mission was distilled in a phrase, "Nourishing the Quality of Life." As the handbook describes it, "To nourish is to keep something alive and well with food. Food is our business and our passion.... We all seek a life that is meaningful, useful, and happy. By committing ourselves and our business to nourishing the quality of life, we help others. By helping others, we improve ourselves. Our business is an opportunity to positively impact the lives of other people—customers and associates."

Passionate about his employees' self-empowerment and personal development, Don retained a consultant named Amba Gale. Amba conducted a myriad of workshops and seminars helping employees cope with conflicts in their lives, fulfill commitments they'd made, and more fully express themselves. "I conducted workshops at each store to help employees nourish the quality of their own lives," Amba says.

Don then hired workshop leader John Wood to develop a consciousness of inspired leadership within the company. Wood crafted a proprietary training agenda for employees, called Learning & Leadership, addressing organizational development, communications, team building, and accountability. More than 160 employees have graduated from the program, including the company's board of directors.

Why did the company invest in these training programs? Amba Gale supplies the answer: "Don had such a profound regard for people. He wanted to provide the opportunity for a greater future for each of his employees." The initiatives succeeded in cultivating communications and leadership skills, but more importantly they helped inspire employees "to a greater purpose," Amba says.

The company also took aim at developing a company-wide quality initiative. It would be executed at the struggling Shoreline store, which was in the process of evolving into another Central Market. Despite many loyal customers, the store's small size and its position in a depressed shopping center put it at a competitive disadvantage. In the late 1990s, the retail chain Ernst Home Center, a neighbor in the shopping center, filed for Chapter 11 bankruptcy protection, while another neighboring store, Pay 'N Save, declared its intentions to pull out of the shopping center. "With the bigger stores leaving and many small shop spaces vacant, we were the last man standing," says Larry.

Don and Larry approached their primary lender to support the idea of a larger, remodeled store. They cited the success of Central Market in Poulsbo and confidently pointed out that the Aurora Square parking lot was of ample size to handle capacity needs. The bank was not impressed. Neither was Associated Grocers—at first. Don, Larry, and Ron sat down with AG's senior executives, who expressed reservations about their plans.

SHARING OUR STORIES

Sailboat Serves as T&C's Guiding Symbol

Throughout T&C's five decades in operation, its leaders have paid great attention to philosophies of good business practices and employee enrichment. T&C founders Ed, Mo, and John spoke at length to employees and each other about the importance of customer service, and their successor, Don, expanded on these principles with ideas of his own.

While the Japanese terms *gaman*, *umami*, and *kaizen* are central tenets to Town & Country Market's paramount goal of nourishing the quality of life, no symbol has been more prominent in the T&C philosophy than the sailboat.

The sailboat graces store signs, bags, and uniforms, and it is used to illustrate the corporate vision in the company handbook that is given to each new employee. While the three elements of the logo—the mainsail, headsail, and hull—each represent a value, the applications for the sailboat metaphor do not end there.

"Like our stores," the company's employee handbook reads, "the ship has a purpose and a destination . . . and like sailboats—with different designs, sails, and rigging that acknowledge the different seas and conditions in which their crews sail—our stores differ from one another."

The handbook likens the many positions throughout the company to those of a sailboat crew: "You must work at your individual task and remember its place in the overall task of sailing the ship, knowing that you are important to the success of the voyage, both as a member of the crew and as an individual."

The metaphor is rounded out with images of customer wants and needs as the driving force that fills the company's sails and exceptional service as its guiding star, "to cross the horizon to that distant shore of total customer satisfaction."

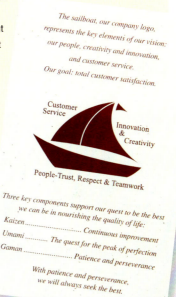

"Just as we were adjourning the meeting, the bookkeeper from the Pay 'N Save store next door came in and mentioned they were closing down," says Jim Huffman, director of the Shoreline market at the time. "T&C immediately began the process to take over that store and others in the shopping center going out of business, including a tropical fish store and a Hallmark." The negotiations with the various store owners proved successful, and AG ultimately backed the strategy and provided the necessary financing.

The goal was not to recreate Poulsbo's Central Market in Shoreline. The objective of the company-wide quality initiative was to take the concept of a fresh destination store much further in Seattle. In charge of facilitating discussions about the quality project was Ron Nakata, although he credits the success of the project to his team. "For

the first time we dwelt on what we didn't want to be and how we could more fully express our essence," Ron says.

Many innovative ideas sprang from the group. While Poulsbo Central Market offered a display just inside the store entrance, the items typically were inexpensive groceries like Western Family Q-Tips. "Instead, we wanted fresh seafood to be one of the first things shoppers saw, which is an absolute no-no in the business," Ron says. "The industry perspective is you don't do that—people aren't ready to buy seafood when they walk in the door. But we felt otherwise and the concept has been a winner."

Another idea was to think of different fresh foods as individual markets. Seattle's famed Pike Place Market inspired the team to think more deeply about the concept of fresh as it related to consumers. "As we identified the mission, we said, 'How can we express fresh to its fullest extent in each department?'" Ron notes. "When we hit the deli, we leaped two evolutionary steps."

Vocabulary also was important to the team in its deliberations. "What was key, we felt, were the words chosen to describe what we sought—that and grounding ourselves in a collaborative process," says Ron. "We saw the experience as a journey, which still continues."

The initiative successfully coalesced employees' energies toward a distinct objective: providing the freshest produce, meat, seafood, and other perishable commodities. Once the designs for the new market were finalized, finding a title to define the result for customers was challenging. The group broke into table groups for discussion, and kept refining different combinations of words to arrive at the simplest, most meaningful, memorable, and distinctive phrase describing what the store stood for. The task culminated in the words "Celebrating Fresh," coined by team member and produce manager Jim Foley.

"Celebrating Fresh" was introduced to the public at the new Shoreline Central Market in January 2000. The store boasted 57,500 square feet of space, nearly double the former size. Customers at the grand opening pressed cell phones to their ears to call friends and relatives and urge them to get in their cars and drive to the store. A ten-thousand-square-foot produce section greeted customers, as did a fifty-two-foot-long meat service counter and a food court featuring Asian and Mexican food operators.

Affixed to the store's exterior was a large, corrugated metal silo printed with the words "Central Market," and a ring circling the top that said "Shoreline." The cylinder also featured the sailboat logo and was crowned by a weather vane. It was Ron's brainchild. "While driving in Silverdale, I saw a silo and thought, here we were creating this vision of 'Celebrating Fresh,' and what says 'fresh' more than a farm and a silo," he recalls. "To me it was a symbol of 'getting closer to the source.'"

Like many of his predecessors, it was by innovating the industry not following its standards that Ron Nakata (left, shown speaking with his cousin Gene Nakata) shaped the Celebrating Fresh concept into a winner for the new Shoreline Central Market, opposite. By bringing fresh seafood, meat, and produce to the front of the store, Ron's concept truly expressed the company's commitment to remaining closer to the source.

4:26 PM

SHORELINE CENTRAL MARKET

Seafood supplier Scott Kimmel stocks saltwater tanks with live Dungeness crabs. Scott's largest crabs are reserved for Town & Country's stores, whose customers have come to expect premium product.

Ron and Don weren't alone in their estimation of the new store. When eventual store director Joel Larway, a former schoolteacher who'd managed a Safeway, walked into the store for the first time, "I couldn't believe what I was seeing," he says. "There were cement floors, a feeling of family-like togetherness, and this profound emphasis on fresh. The produce, seafood, and meat were unbelievable. It just blew me away. I realized I had found the place I wanted to be."

Although the remodeled store experienced the customary J-Curve, its business eventually turned up, and it became financially successful. Customers from Seattle to as far north as Edmonds and east to Lake Forest Park flocked to the new store, drawn by the fresh produce, meat, seafood, and the overall shopping experience. The store hosted entertaining events like "Friday Nights at the Market," a barbecue with entertainment provided by local musicians. It featured seafood extravaganzas and a pumpkin-growing contest for Halloween that yielded a 1,200-pound pumpkin displayed at the store's entrance.

The store also joined its sister markets in sponsoring charitable and philanthropic activities, such as the "Race for the Cure." Ellen Nakata, a breast cancer survivor, had rallied the company in this regard. She and fellow employees Su Reith and Robin Shearer, customers, and friends have come together through the years to walk or run in the annual race sponsored by the Susan G. Komen for the Cure, a breast cancer foundation.

The silo is more than a totem. Within it resides a Caffè Appassionato coffee shop, which provides tables and chairs for al fresco sipping. The silo proved such a distinctive feature that it was adopted by the other Central Markets.

At the grand opening, food moved fast from the sushi bar, the demo kiosks, the pizzeria, and the deli. A blues band warmed up visitors as they shopped. For Don, it was a welcome end to a long journey. "The buzz is very good," he said.

Ron has his own memories: "I remember walking with Don through the store when it was finally finished, and we looked at each other and were both crying. We were blown away by what we were seeing, and at the same time were just so excited. Both of us realized this was something we had to take to other parts of the state, that it represented the future."

In 1995, the year that she was diagnosed with breast cancer, and every year since, Ellen Nakata, right, along with friends Lilly Ransdell (left) and Kay Jensen (center) has led a company-sponsored team for the Susan G. Komen for the Cure. Above: Susan Calhoun, a longtime checker at T&C on Bainbridge Island, has donated a handmade quilt each year since 2002 to be auctioned off with the proceeds going to the Komen foundation.

In September 2000, she and Don were presented with the Komen foundation's Community Hero Award for their efforts on behalf of the organization. This special award in Ellen and Don's names is presented each year to a new recipient. In 2001, the 1,014-member T&C team was the largest ever to participate in this event.

In 2000, Don was basking in the success of the Shoreline grand opening, as well as enjoying his rich family life. Once or twice a week, he devoted time to his first grandchild, Katy, driving her to meetings and store visits. "I'd call him on the phone and he'd say, 'Hold on, Katy needs something,'" says Rolly Radwick. "It said so much about Don and his relationship to family and people."

The many years of managing the company had taken their toll, however. Following a business trip to Europe, Don suffered chest pains. In June 2000, he underwent quadruple heart bypass surgery. After the surgery he felt so well that he jumped over a small fence at Safeco Field, home of his beloved Seattle Mariners baseball team, much to Ellen's consternation. Don recuperated during a needed vacation with Ellen in Louisiana that October. On this trip, Don and Ellen enjoyed an evening of Cajun food, a mint julep, and dancing. That night Don closed his eyes and never opened them again, the victim of a massive stroke. His death was an earthquake that shook his friends deeply and reverberated throughout the company.

SHARING OUR STORIES

Town & Country Employees Remember Compassionate, Inspiring Leader

People who have met Don Nakata never forget the experience. As compassionate as he was passionate, Don left a mark on all who knew him. As his uncle Jerry Nakata says, "He treated everyone the same way, whether they were the president of the local company or the guy sweeping the floors."

Educated at Seattle University, Don pursued two academic paths that merged in his lifetime—business and philosophy. He was a visionary business leader who believed firmly in the personal development of all who worked with him. He was a voracious reader, not just of business titles but of books about diverse subjects. Whenever he found a book personally enriching, he bought several copies and passed them on to friends.

How many CEOs travel to and from business meetings with a sleeping infant in the backseat of his car? Again, Don found a way to weave his business responsibilities into the fabric of his life, squiring his granddaughter Katy around every Monday while her parents worked.

Don also was the kind of Socratic leader who never told employees what to do; instead, he would ask questions that helped them figure out a course on their own. "Don always made you feel comfortable to be around him," says his younger brother Vern Nakata. "You did what he did by watching his actions."

"Everything Don did was on behalf of the customer," says his wife, Ellen Nakata. "He believed that shopping should be a rewarding, fun experience and not a chore. There is no doubt in my mind that he succeeded in this."

He succeeded because he was able to instill in employees his own love of people. "Don treated everyone he had ever met as if they were the most interesting people he knew," says Rolly Radwick, the company's insurance agent. "And this was passed down to the staff."

When Don passed away in 2000, the many people whose lives he'd enriched traded stories of his impact. Su Reith, a checker at Town & Country on Bainbridge, recalled the time she unexpectedly ran into Don at the store early one morning and startled him. "I thought you were God talking to me," Don said. Su replied, "Don, you are the only man I know who could believe God was a woman."

CHAPTER FIVE

New Horizons

Larry Nakata succeeded Don as president of the company. In his wisdom Don had prepared him and others to carry on in the event of his retirement, although it was unimaginable they would be called upon so soon. "I never felt Don would totally retire from the company," says Larry. "When Susan called me that morning to tell me that it was very serious and that she and Julie were flying down right away, I just couldn't believe it."

Don Nakata's legacy is profound, yet his impact extends well beyond the company he shepherded. At his memorial service, his friends and colleagues, many of whom had expressed their feelings about him in cards and letters during his recuperation from heart surgery, spoke of his incomparable love of people. "Business was always second to Don; his family always came first, and everyone who met him felt like part of this family," says Mike Latham.

When Don talked to someone, "he made them feel as if they were the most important person in the room," says Vern Nakata. "You'd never know he was the CEO of a company because he never put himself on a pedestal."

The Nakata family believes Don's spirit is still with them. At important family occasions, they often spy a lone bald eagle, a bird Don loved. "It happens quite a lot," says Julie Bowman, Don and Ellen's daughter. "One time we were all sitting on my mom's deck and an eagle perched on a tree right near us and just stared. Another time my husband got a job promotion, and when he looked out his office window, an eagle flew by."

To honor the memory of Don Nakata, the company annually sponsors the Don Nakata Kaizen Scholarship, which provides funding to employees pursuing continuing education.

This was a challenging time in the company's history. "Everyone was at such an emotional loss with Don's passing," recalls Larry. "The Shoreline store was new, needing time to mature and gain financial stability."

Intelligent and articulate, Larry has a demeanor that reminds many of John Nakata. He is a deliberative person who thinks deeply before he speaks or acts. His financial background and analytical mind had complemented Don's visionary, risk-taking leadership. The task before Larry was to grow the company while improving its operational efficiency, an assignment he pursued with exactitude and vigor. "In very short order, Larry gained the trust and confidence of everyone he worked with," says insurer Rolly Radwick.

For many years the Town & Country philosophy had embraced team-building and collaboration. Looking toward the future, it was clear that more responsibility and accountability would be required of the management team than ever before. In February 2001 the board of

In the new millennium with a new leader, Town & Country Markets would grow to encompass three Central Market stores, in addition to its markets in Ballard, Greenwood, and on Bainbridge Island. At the same time, the company turned back to its roots, acquiring the Nakata family property, opposite, for use as an organic farm. Right: A Daruma doll, or Japanese wish doll, from the Shoreline Central Market. The staff colored in one of the doll's white eyes when it set a financial goal for the store. When the goal is met, they will fill in the other eye.

> For the first time, Larry explained to the group what the total company profits were forecast to be in the coming year. The figures were so marginal that peoples' mouths dropped.

directors—which consisted of Ron Nakata, Wayne Loverich, Greg Johnson, Susan Allen, and Larry Nakata—gathered the store directors and the corporate specialist team for a meeting at the Bainbridge Library. For the first time, Larry explained to the group what the total company profits were forecast to be in the coming year. The figures were so marginal that peoples' mouths dropped. One of the store directors, Steve Williams, remarked, "Why are we even in business?"

That was when the board presented a new procedure, dubbed CAP for Company Action Planning. For the next two months, the board would meet individually with the store directors to review every aspect of their operations and seek ways to manage costs while growing sales. Depending on the size of the store, this exercise took anywhere from half a day to two full days. New targets and commitments were agreed upon.

At the end of the process, another meeting was held in the company meeting room. Here, the new financial goals were shared with the same group that had gathered at the library: the figures considerably exceeded the original. "We were on the same page, unified in our commitment to achieve our goals," reflects Larry. That year, 2001, proved to be a banner one for the company financially.

REFINED IDENTITIES

As the company regained its financial footing, change was in the air. To present a cohesive brand image to customers, the stores ended their long association with the Thriftway marketing platform in 2002. The stores would be branded either a Town & Country Market or a Central Market, creating "a continuity of message that would be easily identifiable to customers," says Brad Lindsey, the company's director of sales and merchandising. Even the corporation received a name change—though a subtle one. On August 23, 2002, just one week shy of the company's forty-fifth anniversary, the corporate name was changed to Town & Country Markets, Inc. The plural spelling reflected the multiple stores under the Town & Country umbrella.

With Don's recent passing coupled with dire financial news, the board, pictured left with Don (center) and controller Cindy Schneider (left of Don), had to find a way to move the company forward. Ron Nakata, Larry Nakata, Susan Allen, Wayne Loverich, and Greg Johnson, (left to right) instituted new procedures that helped turn an emotionally and financially difficult year into one of the most successful in the company's history.

The Big Board, left, is predicated on offering shoppers bargains in produce, meats, seafood, and other perishable items that are so temptingly fresh that customers simply must be informed of their availability.

Other vitally significant changes included the institution of cross-store meetings, an idea developed by Ron Nakata and his team of retail specialists. These were quarterly meetings, often facilitated by Ron, John Wood, and the specialist, with department managers from all the stores. Annual retreats for the entire senior leadership team were also introduced. These meetings would remain critical components in the company's efforts to bring unification among the stores while maintaining their individuality to best serve their markets.

Within each market the Big Board, a large sign placed near the entrance to attract customer attention to "red-hot buys," made its debut. "Big Board is all about fresh—a fabulous array of the freshest tiger prawns or peak-of-the-season grapes," Lindsey explains. "Unlike other stores, you're not going to see Tide detergent or Cheerios up front."

These various changes and strategies were directly influenced by employees. "They're the ones close to the customer and our markets," says Ron. He believes the emphasis on collaborative input explains the company's low attrition rate when compared to other retail grocers.

Each store evolved according to the tastes and needs of their respective communities. T&C unveiled a new floral pavilion, upstairs deck and enclosed foyer made of glass and concrete columns. Poulsbo Market Place underwent yet another name change to Town & Country Poulsbo Market. In 2002, the store hosted its third annual "Tropical Daze" luau. At nearby Central Market, local "hot rodders" and classic car buffs showcased their vehicles in the parking lot at "Cruz Nite" celebrations. Weekend barbecues, pig roasts, and "Bratwurst Days" were other fun events. The latter called for sausage grilling on a mass scale by the Johnsonville Touring Grill, the world's largest rolling barbecue.

Ballard Market also dusted off major renovations in April 2003. The old working-class neighborhood had become more economically and culturally diverse. It was a favored nesting ground for young singles and couples working in Seattle's booming technology industry, comprising such high-tech pioneers as Microsoft and Amazon.com. To appeal to these new customers, the front of the

12:31 AM

POULSBO CENTRAL MARKET

Steve Habner squeegees a stainless steel table in the meat cutting room. Each night Habner cleans all of the meat cutting equipment, hoses down the floors, and sterilizes all surfaces so that the next day's processing is done in a pristine environment.

market was pushed out fifteen feet to form an appealing new entry that maximized the natural light, while the interior was expanded to accommodate a twice-as-big produce section. "The neighborhood was changing into a younger, trendier clientele that was really into cooking, so we decided to focus on 'organics' and 'fresh' by expanding the perimeter seafood, meat, deli, and food service departments," says store director Steve Williams. "While we changed the physical building, we didn't touch its soul."

The store remained a beacon, even though the giant awning that had been visible from the sky was torn down. In its stead was an equally imposing series of four-foot-tall letters spelling out the store's name. On hand for the Ballard Market's grand re-opening was none other than Stan Boreson, the accordion-playing humorist who'd tossed tokens from a helicopter at T&C's debut forty-six years earlier.

Greenwood Market also was remodeled to accommodate a larger produce section and was given signage reminiscent of the other company stores. The market retained its scrappiness but in a nostalgic sense. "This store is all about *gaman*," says Larry. "It's a true neighborhood market—proof that bigger isn't necessarily better."

Long a neighborhood icon, Ballard Market, above, underwent a major renovation in 2003 to appeal to the newcomers nesting in the old Scandinavian enclave. The red awning that beckoned shoppers from afar was replaced with equally imposing neon letters standing tall above a new storefront. Below: An early Ballard Market apron patch with the familiar sailboat logo.

Although small by other company store standards, Greenwood Market, right, is the true essence of a neighborhood market. Because of its small size and loyal customer base, employees know many customers by name, and it is common to see mothers with children in strollers or older customers who have been shopping at the location for years taking afternoon walks to the market, to purchase something for lunch or dinner, for sure, but also to chat with friends and neighbors.

CONTINUING TO INSPIRE

On a recent visit to the store, Larry could be seen assisting store director Patty Nolan bagging groceries and hauling them out to shoppers' cars. The customers had no idea that it was the CEO of Town & Country Markets, Inc. who was carrying their bags. "Whenever he's here, that's what he does," says Patty. "We talk about the store while he bags and I check."

Like Don, Larry has set a tone for his fellow employees, who are inspired at all times to follow the "Eleven Commandments of Good Business," which are listed in the company handbook. Among these tenets is, "The customer deserves the most courteous and attentive service we can provide."

One provider of that courteous and attentive service is Jacqui Carpenter, a bright, articulate woman who is passionate about her work managing natural and bulk foods at Ballard Market. "I find it stimulating to sell a variety of fresh natural foods that haven't been sitting around in a box for months, as well as an abundant assortment of exotic dried fruits like strawberries and wild blueberries—little treats, I call them," she says.

Jacqui envisions her job as an opportunity to interact with customers to achieve personal growth and self-discovery. "I care about the people who shop at our store," she says. "They pull up in their cars and make a decision to come here for a reason. I am honored to work for a company that is so humane, that takes the human condition into consideration at all times. We are alive here. We are aware."

Thanks to the fervor and commitment of employees, Town & Country Markets, Inc. was again on strong financial footing. Revenues and profits were up, and the time was ripe to build a third Central Market. In mid-2002, the board of directors toured a future master-planned community in the city of Mill Creek, a relatively affluent region twenty miles north of Seattle. For years, the city's planners had held onto a large parcel of land to develop it into something special. Their plan now was to build a massive town center, the modern equivalent of a quaint downtown with homes, stores, and tree-lined sidewalks.

Two anchor tenants were sought for the proposed town center. University Books, an independent bookseller, was named as one anchor. Thanks to real estate consultant Dorrie Johnson, Central Market was being considered for the other. Dorrie had assisted the company

SHARING OUR STORIES

"Uncle Jerry" Celebrates Unprecedented Four-Decade Run at T&C

Every family should have an Uncle Jerry. Jerry Nakata was the last remaining son of Jitsuzo and Shima Nakata. His entire life had been spent in the grocery business, from the days assisting his oldest brother, John, at Charley Bremer's Eagle Harbor Market. Jerry marked his fortieth year at T&C shortly before his death in June of 2007, when colleagues and customers remembered his sharp wit and all-around fun spirit.

Jerry spent World War II at the Manzanar Relocation Center and another internment camp, Minidoka, in Idaho. He tried to enlist like his brother Mo but was declared "4F." After the war, he joined John at the Paramount grocery in Seattle and then took over running the store when John left to restart Eagle Harbor Market on Bainbridge. Jerry returned to the island to manage the tiny Lynwood Market. Duncan West, a customer at the market in the 1960s, fondly recalls Jerry at this time. "The Nakata family installed Judd Huney, a former owner [of the store], as a butcher," West says. "That was a double win, as Judd was one of the world's friendliest butchers, and Jerry Nakata continued Judd's policy of allowing kids to charge candy to their parents' accounts."

Stories about Jerry abound. During his unscheduled job interview with Jerry at Viking Mark-It, Greg Johnson, who didn't have a resume with him, was asked to write out his experience on a lunch-sized paper bag. That was good enough. Without hesitation, Jerry hired him, and they worked together for years before Greg went into computers and software development for the company.

"Uncle Jerry had a great sense of humor—he was always making people laugh," says Larry Nakata. "He was beloved by all and was an invaluable part of our culture and the values we hold dear. Even into his semi-retirement years, Jerry was still making a huge contribution. He was one in a million."

in obtaining a long-term lease at Ballard Market, a process that took seven years. In June 2002, she took the T&C team on a tour of four sites for a new Central Market; it was Mill Creek Town Center that seemed right. "It fit perfectly with what we wanted," says Larry. T&C immediately signed a lease to operate the new store by the end of August 2004.

VOTE OF CONFIDENCE

In the ensuing period, he and Jim Huffman, designated store director for the new Central Market, met with the Mill Creek City Council, which knew little about the company or its stores. Larry explained the differences between a Central Market and other supermarkets. He explained the company's philosophy of "Nourishing the Quality of Life" and the "Celebrating Fresh" concept. He pointed out that the meat department in the new store would be like the meat markets of old. After Larry was done, a tall, elderly gentleman on the council stood up and spoke very softly. He mentioned that when he was a boy, he used to go to a butcher shop on Bainbridge Island owned by a fellow named John Nakata.

"He said it was his favorite butcher shop of all time, and that Johnny was one of the finest people he'd ever met," says Larry. "He then turned to his fellow council members and said, 'This is a good company. I personally know the Nakata and Loverich families and can tell you they are the

A mouth-watering display of cheeses from around the globe is just one of the many splendid delights awaiting customers at the Mill Creek Central Market's deli, left. Wayne Loverich, longtime T&C store director on Bainbridge Island and currently a member of the board, had the prescience years ago to realize the attraction of a world-class deli at each of the company's stores.

best of the best.' You could hear a pin drop. I couldn't believe it. It was very moving. We couldn't have asked for a better or more personal endorsement."

The gentleman's name is Jack Start. Unbeknownst to Larry at the time, when he was a child, the Starts lived across the street from the Nakatas, and Jack played baseball at Bainbridge High.

The third Central Market opened for business in September 2004. Approximately 1,200 guests attended the grand opening, previewing the food, facilities, and staff. The layout was similar to Central Market in Shoreline, with a large produce section on the left, bordered by the meat and seafood departments, and a grocery section within. But the 56,500-square-foot store sported an entirely new look in food service.

The deli took people's breath away. Not only was it extremely large by comparison with other stores, it was an epicure's delight. Thanks in large part to Wayne Loverich and the Food Service Team, the selection of specialty foods was diverse and mouth-watering. Not one, but four different kinds of fresh mozzarella floated in water. It is impossible to walk by the cold entrée bar, the large hot case, the long cheese wall, or the antipasto bar and not want to sample the fare. "The deli was like a beehive through the morning and the lunch hour," *Compass*, the company's newsletter, reported.

Produce was stacked on wooden pallets to give shoppers the feel of a country market. The meat department promoted its "aged beef program" and featured a so-called "bloom box" separating the cutting area from the front service area. Then there's the seafood department, right there as you enter the front door, with live crab, oyster, fish, clam, and lobster tanks on view. "This store was a dream come true," Larry commented in the *Compass*. "Hundreds of people, within and outside the company, made this possible, and they all should be congratulated."

END OF AN ERA

As the new store made its debut, T&C Poulsbo Market breathed its last. The lease was about to expire on the thirty-year-old market and the fees to extend the lease were much higher. The company also braced for a 210,000-square-foot

5:20 PM

SHORELINE CENTRAL MARKET

Customer Rene Dickey picks up ingredients for dinner on her way home from work. The city of Shoreline's largest age demographic is made up of people between the ages of twenty-five and forty-four, and the growing segment of young professionals is reflected in the store's after-work rush.

Longtime shoppers and veteran employees comforted each other at the closing of the Poulsbo Market, left. Local newspapers covered the closure on their front pages. The *North Kitsap Herald,* lamenting the closure, noted that the market "had gained itself a loyal following [and had] been known as a center for community activity." Below: The store's first customer and owner of the land that the store was built on, Gladys Paulson, greets Greg Johnson at the farewell party. Behind her is the store's former director and current Town & Country Markets, Inc. president Larry Nakata.

Wal-Mart Supercenter set to open nearby. "We knew we could no longer operate two stores in the same market area," Larry says.

Store employees had nine months to prepare for the closure. Nearly all found assignments at other company stores. Nevertheless, during the final days employees and longtime customers traded hugs and tearful good-byes. Letters from shoppers flowed in to local newspapers and the company's newsletter. "I don't leave the store these days without a lump in my throat," a woman wrote to *Compass.* The *North Kitsap Herald* newspaper covered the closing in several front page stories. "It is a store that gained itself a loyal following," one article commented, "evidenced by the large groups of shoppers and lunch-time gatherings still taking place one week from the final day."

On the store's last day in business, Susan Allen, Ron Nakata, and Wayne Loverich worked as checkers. Ten employees, including store director Al Moore, displayed tattoos of the Japanese symbol for "friendship," which they had gotten to commemorate the store's closing and their personal kinship. A ragtime band was on hand to entertain the packed house. Shoppers perused photos and other memorabilia dating to the market's opening in 1974. "First Customer" Gladys Paulson was present to share her memories, wearing the same outfit she'd worn three decades before. "When I came in the door and saw how bare the shelves were, I almost cried," Gladys told the *North Kitsap Herald*.

As Town & Country Markets, Inc. neared its fiftieth anniversary in 2007, many within the organization reflected on the lessons of the past half century. Mo, Ed, and John had established the company's foundations of relatedness and connectedness with the community. "The founders were role models," says Susan Allen, John's granddaughter and a member of the fourth generation of Nakatas to live on American soil.

In this story of two families and the deeply personal company they created, America figured prominently. Jitsuzo Nakata and Tom Loverich were men who dreamed of a better life in a better place for themselves and their families. This country gave them opportunities they never forgot. They were patriots whose children and grandchildren served our armed forces. One need look no further than the table Jitsuzo carved in

SHARING OUR STORIES

Customer Appreciates Care, Concern Shown to Family

David Guterson, author of the best-selling novel *Snow Falling on Cedars*, which is inspired by events that took place on Bainbridge, moved to the island in 1984 with his wife and three sons to teach high school. On a Saturday morning nearly twenty years ago, his wife, Robin, parked her 1967 International Travelall in T&C's parking lot. As she exited the vehicle with her two-year-old son in her arms, the car "began to roll backward, slowly, down the parking lot grade," Guterson recalls. "My wife leaned in to press down the parking brake with her free hand. Then the moving door frame struck her, and she fell backward. The back of my wife's head and our two-year-old son's face hit the pavement."

The Travelall rolled over Robin's right leg, leaving tire marks on it before crossing her pelvis. The vehicle then rolled toward the store with the other boys in it, coming to rest against one of the heavy posts beside the stairs to the wine cellar and bulk foods department. "When I got to T&C that morning, there were a couple hundred people in the parking lot," Guterson says. "There were also two aid cars, one for my two-year-old son and one for my wife. They were both going to Harborview [Medical Center]. I went with them on the ferry, alternating between those aid cars. Then I alternated between them at the hospital."

The next morning it was clear that his wife and son were going to be all right. David returned home with his other sons, making a brief stop at T&C on the way. "The Travelall was gone—T&C had seen to getting it towed," he says. "The post in front was damaged, [but] nobody at T&C ever said a word to me about insurance, liability, repairs, legal responsibility, or money. They only asked repeatedly about the health of my family. I was a young high school teacher then living in a rental house with three young children and a lot of bills to pay. I was worried about the costs associated with this accident. So I have never forgotten how T&C treated us after our accident. That's what T&C is about. Its heart, every day, is in the right place."

For twenty-three years, the Gutersons have shopped at Town & Country, and they are not about to stop. "We are treated not only with kindness there but friendship," David says. "The spirit of the place is, for us, the spirit of Bainbridge. T&C is part of what we mean in our family when we use the word 'home.'"

1:20 PM

MILL CREEK CENTRAL MARKET

Produce clerk Holiday Karr straightens rows of ripe bananas. In addition to carrying popular national brands like Chiquita bananas, Town & Country Markets works with small, local suppliers, giving customers a range of choice.

The two-story farmhouse, top, that Jitsuzo and Shima Nakata purchased in 1924 sprouts from the working strawberry farm. Above: Young members of the Nakata clan play baseball in the fields surrounding the farmhouse. Thanks to its acquisition by T&C in 2001, the newly christened MiddleField Farm, opposite, will be preserved for future generations to enjoy, supplying organic fruits and vegetables to T&C stores.

the Manzanar internment camp, the legs made from desert brush, to describe his love for his adopted land.

"Each chapter in our family's history happened on American soil," says Wayne Nakata. "Despite setbacks, losses, hardships, and interruptions in their lives, our family still found fertile ground on which to make a living, to raise children, and to live comfortably with friends in a community that offered singular opportunities for a good life."

PRESERVING THE PAST

In October 2001, Town & Country Markets bought the original property (approximately thirteen acres) from the sons of John and Pauline Nakata and their heirs for preservation of the land. While many possibilities were discussed, one use, in particular, held the most interest—that was a return to farming. "To me the farm represents who we are," says Vern Nakata. "It is our roots. It is where we grew up as kids. Its preservation will give meaning for all who follow."

After several years of soil replenishment, Brian McWhorter of Butler Green Farms, a longtime organic farmer and friend on Bainbridge Island and regular supplier to T&C's produce department, was hired to transition the farm back to life.

Planting a few acres at a time, Brian has grown zucchini, corn, beans, squash, pumpkins, and even sunflowers. Each picking is brought to either the Winslow store or to the Poulsbo Central Market for quick sale in the produce and floral departments. "The Nakata family philosophically believes that it is important for people to know where their food comes from," says McWhorter. "They also believe it

The smiling faces on these pages belong to the people who work for Town & Country Markets, Inc.'s six stores. They and their predecessors during the past half century said "good morning" to customers, took care of their little ones while they ran off to get that forgotten quart of milk, provided delicious food samples, responded to questions, listened to customer needs and stories, and, like the three founders, really cared.

is important for future generations of their family to understand the heritage of this island as a farm community. They're doing their best to support local farmers—what's left of them—and maintain the rural character of Bainbridge by saving the farmland."

Ultimately the company's vision for the farm is to contribute in new ways to the broader community of its employees, current and future family members, and residents of Bainbridge Island as a whole.

For its employees, the farm may house a learning center where meetings, classes, and new employee orientations could take place, along with a firsthand look at how food is grown and harvested. For the community, it would be a pleasant respite. And for family members, the farm would be a place to return to—the place where it all began in America.

"Even though this company has gotten bigger, the farm is there to remind us who we are and how we started," says Glen Nakata. "It represents the circle of life."

The options for the land are numerous, but one thing is certain—the name. In Japanese, *Naka* means "middle," while *ta* means "field," leading the Nakata family to believe that their ancestry includes a legacy of farmers—ancestors who used land to provide sustenance for their families. Therefore, the company has determined that one day there will be a sign on the property that proclaims the farm "MiddleField Farm."

And nearby in the town of Winslow, on the same lot where kids of different languages played pickup baseball games, stands the Town & Country Market. Even with the changes of the past and expected changes for the future, the store still evokes the same spirit that was evident on its first day in business fifty years ago.

SPIRIT OF SERVICE

Kay Nakao, who appears two decades younger than her nearly ninety years, still shops regularly at T&C. It is the highlight of her day. "Many people still remember me, which makes me feel so special," she says, fondly looking at the location of her old checkout stand, surely musing about the tots she cuddled as their moms chased to the back to grab a container of milk.

Bainbridge islander and former Washington Secretary of State Ralph Munro says, "I can still remember with fondness Johnny and Mo cutting the meat, Ed Loverich at the cash register, Kay Nakao and Fudge Sakuma at the checkout stands." Ralph, who was there on the grand opening day in August 1957 when he was fourteen, reflects, "Everyone there was so good to all of us kids.

"And they still are."

LOVERICH FAMILY TREE

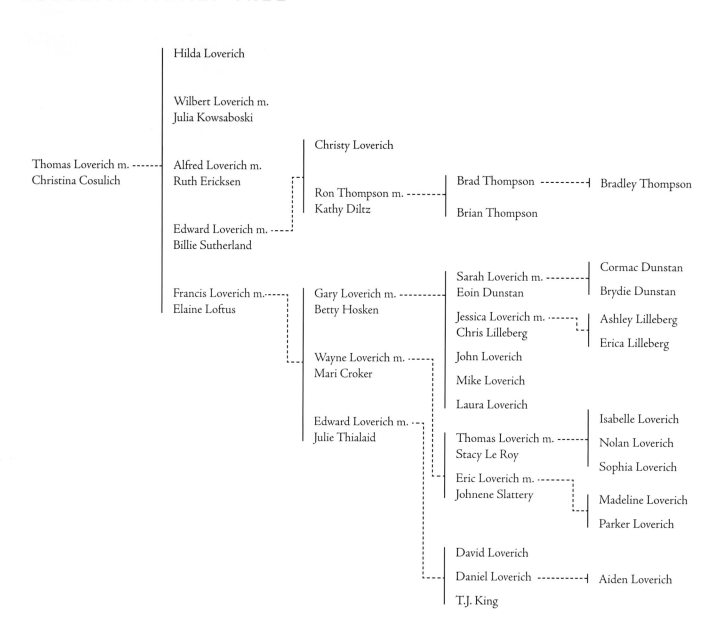

NAKATA FAMILY TREE

Jitsuzo Nakata m. Shima Akimoto

- Masaaki "John" Nakata m. Yukiye "Pauline" Kawamoto
  - Donald Nakata m. Ellen Naruto
    - Susan Nakata m. Ronald Allen
      - Katherine Allen
      - Natalie Allen
    - Julie Nakata m. Robert "David" Bowman
      - Matthew Bowman
      - Rachel Bowman
    - Anthony Nakata m. April Whitney
      - Whitney Nakata
    - David Nakata m. Nichelle "Nikki" Lindberg
      - Ashley Nakata
      - Brandon Nakata
      - Colten Nakata
      - Hope Nakata
  - Robert Nakata m. Sally Shimizu
    - Lindsey Nakata
  - Wayne Nakata m. Judith Campbell
  - Vernon Nakata m. Amy Horio

- Shigeko "Jean" Nakata Kawamoto m. Joseph Kawamoto
  - Ray Kawamoto m. Marguerite Kennison
    - Robert "Tony" Kawamoto
    - Heather Kawamoto
    - Jeanna Kawamoto
      - Kayleigh Kawamoto

- Kikuyo Nakata

- Yoshie "Yonchan" Nakata m. Kyoichi "Doc" Iwasa
  - Ralph Iwasa m. Diane Wada
  - Lynn Iwasa m. Meredith Linstrom
    - Karen Iwasa m. Mike Lubofsky
    - Joy Iwasa
    - Kenneth Iwasa
    - Bradley Iwasa
    - Douglas Iwasa

- Haruye Nakata

- Sadako "Sa" Nakata m. Takeo "Joe" Kodani
  - April Kodani m. Richard Numamoto
    - Jason Numamoto
    - Dana Numamoto

- Nakata Girl

- Momoichi "Mo" Nakata m. Sachiko "Sa" Koura
  - Larry Nakata m. Alexandra "Sandy" Naylor
  - Daniel Nakata
  - Ronald Nakata m. Susan Hawkins
    - Kara Nakata m. Henry Van Voorhis
    - Reid Nakata
  - Martin Nakata

- Gerald "Jerry" Nakata m. Sueko "Sue" Terayama
  - Gerald Nakata, Jr. m. Yuka Ohara
  - Richard "Rick" Nakata
  - Kathleen Nakata
  - Glen Nakata m. Gail Stanley
    - Bonnie Nakata m. Richard Matcho
      - London Matcho
    - Edward Nakata
    - Kristi Nakata
  - Gene Nakata
  - Steven Nakata
  - Janis Nakata
  - Leslie Nakata m. Donald Stimson
    - Alison Nakata
    - Megan Nakata

- Kenneth Nakata m. Yoshiko "Yo" Kitayama
  - Karen Nakata
  - Cheryl Nakata m. Aaron Paston
  - Irene Nakata m. Curtis Endow
    - Davis Endow
    - Julia Endow

INDEX

Pages in bold indicate photographs.

A

Aalsmeer Flower Auction, 31, 66
Agenosho, Japan, 13, 18
Albertsons, 67
Allen, Katherine "Katy," 107
Allen, Susan (Nakata)
    birth of, 56
    at T&C, 92
    on the board, **110,** 121
    memories of, 67, 71, 94, 96
Ancich, Jack, 54
Associated Grocers (AG), 46, 49, 57, 59, 60, 67, 70–72, 83, 93, 101

B

Baer, Max, 46, **47,** 49
Bagwandin, Omrao, 82
Bainbridge, William, 14
Bainbridge Gardens, 35, **41,** 42–43, 51
Bainbridge High School, 20, 27, 50, 117
Bainbridge Investors, Inc., 43
Bainbridge Island, Washington
    as bedroom community to Seattle, 51
    geography of, 14
    history of, 14
    Japanese communities on, 18–19
Ballard Market
    atmosphere of, 59
    awning of, **72,** 73
    "Cruz Nite," 75
    exterior photographs of, **58, 72, 114**
    founding of, 71
    grocery cart drill team of, 75
    interior photographs of, **30–31, 84–85**
    MAP meeting at, **78**
    produce department of, **84–85,** 88–89
    renovation of, 111, **114**
    "Singles Night," **73,** 74
Beck, Tracey, **76**
Beran, Karin, **74**
Big Board, **111**
Biggs, Bryan, 76, **77**
Billings, Gwen, **74**
Borenson, Stan, 46, 114
Bowman, Julie (Nakata), 56, 109
Bremer, Charley, 20, 25, 26, 27, 116
Brooks, Mike, **90,** 91

C

Calhoun, Susan, 64, 75, **106**
CAP (Company Action Planning), 110
Carpenter, Jacqui, 115
Central Market. *See* Mill Creek Central Market; Poulsbo Central Market; Shoreline Central Market
Clark, Irene, **16,** 17
Clark, Margaret, 65, 82–83, **86,** 87
Clarke, Sam, 94, 95
Clifford, Tim, **90,** 91
Cody, Wayne, **70**
Commodore School, 55
Cox, Dale, 82, 93
Creech, Martha, 50
Curtis, Steve, 73

D

Davenport, Al, 51
Davis, Mike, 59
Dickey, Rene, **118–19**
Donegan, Julie, **98,** 99
DW Green Company, 92

E

Eagle Harbor Congregational Church, 20, 78
Eagle Harbor Market, **12,** 13, 20, **21,** 25–27, 32, **33,** 35, 36, 40, 42, 116
Edmundson, Clarence "Hec," 28
Equal Exchange, 87
Excellence in Food Marketing (EFM), 71, 78, 86

F

Farmer's Wholesale Cooperative, 82
Field, Michael, 81
Finley, Steve, 97

Flack, Carolyn, **98,** 99
Foley, Jim, 103
Food Marketing Institute, 83
Fourth of July parade, **74, 75**
Fox, Esther, 32
Fred Meyer, 94

G
Gale, Amba, 100, 101
Gaman, 29, 32, 100, 101, 114
Goller, Lou, 35
Goodwin, Carolyn, 32
Gore, Bruce, **87**
Great Blizzard of 1990, 83
Green, DW, 92–93, 97
Greenwood Market, **22–23, 52–53,** 114, **115**
Greenwood Price Chopper, **88**
Grocery cart drill teams, **75**
Gunning, John, 82
Guterson, David and Robin, 121

H
Habner, Steve, **112–13**
Hall, Tom, 70, 71, 96–97
Hall Brothers Shipyard, **14–15**
Hanlon-Wilde, Tom, 87
Hansen, "Tub," 40
Harris, Fred, 44, **45**
Harui family, 41
Hattaland Partners, 94, 95
Hawaiian Days, 61, **64, 66**
Helpline House, 67
Hendricks, Casey, 41
Herkenrath, Anne, **22–23**
Hoffman, William, 57
Horne, Kathleen, 54
Huffman, Jim, 116

I
IGA, 43, 57
Island Days, 64
Iversen, Sharen, 76, **77**

J
Jackson, Michael, **99**
Japanese Americans, internment of, 35–37, 40
Japanese immigration, 13, 18
Jensen, James, **68**
Jensen, Kay, **106**
Johansen, Bryan, **96,** 97
Johnson, Dorrie, 115
Johnson, Greg, **70,** 78, 86, 88, 92–94, **110,** 116, **120**
Johnson, Russell, 89
Jones, Art, 60, 78

K
Kaizen, 100, 101
Karr, Holiday, **122,** 123
Kawamoto, Joseph, 26, **27**
Kawamoto, Shigeko "Jean" (Nakata), 26, 37
Kelly & Payne, 50
Kimmel, Scott, **104–5**
Klausenburger, Marcus, **52–53**
Klondike Gold Rush, 14, 15
Kodani, Sadako (Nakata), **36,** 37
Kodani, Takeo "Joe," **36**
Kori, Marjorie, **62–63**
Koura, Art, **29,** 35, 37
Koura, Florence (Yoshitake), 37
Koura, Kenso, **29**
Koura, Tony, 37

L
Lamping, Penny, 32
Lamping, Tom, 27
Larry's Market, 86
Larway, Joel, 106
Latham, Mike, 100, 109
Levy, Joel, 81
Lincoln Elementary School, 20, 24
Lindsey, Brad, 110, 111
Losinj (Lussin), Croatia, 14–15

Louis, Joe, 46, **47,** 49
Loverich, Alfred "Fred," 24
Loverich, Billie (Sutherland)
   marries Ed Loverich, 40
   suggests Town & Country name, 46
   at T&C grand opening, 47, **48,** 49
   Hawaiian Days and, 64
   retirement of, 78
   memories of, 41, 42, 51, 64
Loverich, Christina (Cosulich), 13, 15, 20, 24, **25,** 27
Loverich, Christy, 55, 61, **66,** 67
Loverich, Edward "Ashcan"
   childhood of, 24, **25**
   as basketball player, 27, **28,** 100
   in the military, 35, 36
   marries Billie Sutherland, 40
   at Bainbridge Gardens, 35, 41–43
   Town & Country Market founded by, 35, 43, 46–47, **57**
   at T&C, 49, 50, 51, 54, 59, 60, **61**
   as King Kamehameha, **64,** 100
   retirement of, 78
   death of, 100
Loverich, Elaine (Loftus), 47, **48,** 49, 55, 64, 78
Loverich, Francis, 24, **25, 29,** 40, 47
Loverich, Gary, 24, 29, 42, 49, 54
Loverich, Hilda, 20, 24, **25,** 36, 42, 49, 55
Loverich, Mari (Croker), 32, 78, 81
Loverich, Thomas
   immigrates to U.S., 15
   marries Christina Cosulich, 15
   at Hall Brothers Shipyard, **14,** 15
   as fisherman, 20
   at Winslow Dock Grocery, 13, 24, 25, 27
   in retirement, **42**
   death of, 42

Loverich, Wayne
   childhood of, 49
   education of, 55
   in the military, 55
   at T&C, 55, 59, 60, 64, **65**, 81, 86
   on the board, **110**, 117, 121
   memories of, 50, 67, 83
Loverich, Wilbert "Bill," 24, **25**
Loverich family tree, 128
Lucky Stores, 70–71
Luisetti, Hank, 28
Lynwood Market, 49, 116

M
Malko, Gerry, 82
Manzanar Relocation Center, 35, **36**, 37, 40, 116
MAP (Management Action Planning), **76–77**, 78
Mark-It Foods, 59
Martinez, Edgar, 92
McKeel, Craig, **90**, 91
McNulty, "Pinky," 50
McWhorter, Brian, 82, **87**, 124, 126
Meadosweet Dairy Foods, 49
MiddleField Farm, **124, 125**, 126–27
Mill Creek Central Market, 115, 116, **117, 122–23**
Monroe, Russ, 54
Mosquito Fleet, 20, 24, 51
Munro, Ralph, 47, 56, 127

N
Nagaya, Washington, 18–19
Nakao, Kay Sakai
   childhood of, 37
   at Eagle Harbor Market, 33
   at T&C checkout stand, 49, **51**, 55, 66
   Hawaiian Days and, **66**
   retirement of, 66, 127
   memories of, 25, 50, 65
Nakao, Sam, 24, 49, 66
Nakata, Alexandra "Sandy" (Naylor), 55, 59

Nakata, Donald
   birth of, 27
   in internment camp, **36**
   education of, 49, 55, 107
   in the military, 49, **55**
   at T&C, 55, 56, **57, 107, 110**
   marries Ellen Naruto, 55–56
   expansion under, 57, 59–60, 70–73, 78, 86, 88, 92–94
   on European trips, 66, 67
   awards given to, **79**, 107
   in family photo, **100**
   personality of, 107, 109
   vision of, for company, 78, 100–101, 107
   death of, 107, 109

Nakata, Ellen (Naruto), 50, 55–56, 59, 66, 79, **106**, 107
Nakata, Gene, **103**
Nakata, Gerald "Jerry"
   birth of, 20
   at Eagle Harbor Market, 26
   in internment camp, 35, 37, 116
   at Paramount grocery, 42, **43**, 49, 116
   at Lynwood Market, 49, 116
   at Viking Mark-It, 59, 116
   at Poulsbo Market Place, 70, **116**
   memories of, 25, 28, 55
   personality of, 116
   death of, 116
Nakata, Glen, 126
Nakata, Jitsuzo
   immigrates to U.S., 13–14
   barbershop and bathhouse of, 14, 15, 18, **19**, 20
   strawberry farm purchased by, 24–25, 26, 33, 87, **124**
   in internment camp, **36**, 37, 40
   in retirement, **42**
   death of, 42–43
Nakata, Karen, **38**
Nakata, Kenneth
   birth of, 20
   as basketball player, **29**

   in internment camp, **36**, 37
   in the military, 37
   at Bainbridge Gardens, 37
   at T&C, 49, **65**
   Hawaiian Days and, 64
Nakata, Larry
   birth of, 41
   childhood of, 49
   education of, 55, 89
   in the military, 55
   at T&C, 51, 55
   at Viking Mark-It, 59, 67
   at Poulsbo Market Place, 88, **89**
   named "Person of the Year," 92
   at Poulsbo Central Market, 93–96
   as CEO, 109–10, 115, 116, 117, **118**
   memories of, 75, 79, 88, 116
   personality of, 109
Nakata, Masaaki "John"
   birth of, 13, 19
   in high school, 20
   as worker at Eagle Harbor Market, 20, 25–26
   marries Pauline Kawamoto, 26, **27**
   as owner of Eagle Harbor Market, 13, **26**, 32–33
   pays off strawberry farm mortgage, 26, 29, 32
   in internment camp, **36**, 37
   sale of Eagle Harbor Market by, 36, 40
   declines partnership in Bainbridge Gardens, 41
   at Paramount grocery, 42, **43**
   repurchase of Eagle Harbor Market by, 35, 42
   Town & Country Market founded by, 35, 43, 46–47, **57**
   at T&C, 49, 56
   retirement of, 56, 60
   death of, 97, 100
Nakata, Momoichi "Mo"
   birth of, 20
   in high school, 28, **29**

at Eagle Harbor Market, 26, 32
in internment camp, **36,** 37
in the military, 35, 37, 38
marries Sachiko Koura, **40**
at Bainbridge Gardens, 35, **41,** 42, 43
Town & Country Market founded by, 35, 43, 46–47, **57,** 79
at T&C, 49, 56, 60, 61
heart attack of, 56
personality of, 27
death of, 78, 100
Nakata, Robert, **36, 100**
Nakata, Ronald
childhood of, 49
at T&C, 55
at Village Foods, 67
at Poulsbo Market Place, 70, 88
at Shoreline Price Chopper, 86
at Shoreline Central Market, 101, **103,** 106
on the board, **110,** 111, 121
Nakata, Sachiko "Sa" (Koura), 37, **40**
Nakata, Shima
barbershop and bathhouse of, 18, **19**
farm purchased by, 33, **124**
in internment camp, **36,** 37, 40
death of, 42
Nakata, Vernon
birth of, 49
at T&C, 76, **77**
in family photo, **100**
memories of, 51, 59, 70, 107, 109, 124
Nakata, Wayne
birth of, 32
childhood of, **36,** 40, 42
as box boy, **46,** 47, 49
in family photo, **100**
memories of, 18, 25, 32, 33, 59, 124
Nakata, Yukiye "Pauline" (Kawamoto)
marries John Nakata, 26, **27**
at Eagle Harbor Market, 33, 35
in internment camp, **36,** 37
in family photo, **100**
Nakata family tree, 129
Nolan, Patty, 115

O
Olson, Morrie, 79
Overlake Market, 78

P
PAD (Product Awareness through Demonstration), 78
Papineau, Linda, **17**
Paramount grocery, 42, **43,** 49, **116**
Paulson, Clarence, 59
Paulson, Gladys, 59, 119, **120**
Payne, Bob, 50
Pearl Harbor, bombing of, 33, 35
Pedersen, Rick, **76**
Peltier, Louis, 57
Peters, Dave, 94–95
Peters, Tom, 72
Pike Place Market, 61, 67, 97, 103
Port Blakely Lumber Mill, 13, 19
Poulsbo, Washington, 59
Poulsbo Central Market
concept for, 92–94
as destination store, 96
drawing of, **92–93**
events at, 96–97, 111
exterior photograph of, **93**
as green building, 94–95
interior photographs of, **68–69, 95, 96, 98–99, 112–13**
opening of, 94
Poulsbo Market Place, 67, 70, **71,** 75, 79, **89,** 95–96, 111. See also Town & Country Poulsbo Market
Pulicicchio, Joe, 88–89, 93

Q
Queen Anne Thriftway, 66

R
Radwick, Rolly, 83, 107, 109
Ransdell, Lilly, **106**
Reagan, Ronald, 40
Reese, Gary, 81

Reister, Bob, 59
Reith, Su, 106, 107
Renton, William, 13
Rhodes, Dick, 66
Robinson, Kate, **30,** 31
Roosevelt, Franklin Delano, 35

S
Safeway, 61, 79, 81, 83
Sailboat metaphor, 72, 101
Sakai, Paul, 35, 51
Sakuma, Fudge, 127
Salmon Derby, 64
Schneider, Cindy, 88, 97, **110**
Seattle Mariners, 92, 107
Shearer, Robin, 106
Sheehan, Dan, **84,** 85
Sherry, Bob, 88
Shoreline Central Market
events at, 106–7
exterior photographs of, **6–7, 80**
interior photographs of, **62–63, 102, 103, 104–5, 118–19**
opening of, 103, 106
size of, 103
vision for, 81, 101, 103
Shoreline Price Chopper, 86, 97
Short, Ron, 92
Smith, Mrs. "Smitty," 51
Start, Jack, 117
Sumiyoshi family, 24
Suquamish Indians, 14
Susan G. Komen Race for the Cure, 106–7
Sutherland, Bill, 49
Sutherland, Jack, 40

T
Taniguchi, Teruo, 51
Thornton, Don, **76–77**
Thriftway, 43, 46, 47, 61, 67, 110

Town & Country Market on Bainbridge Island
  exterior photographs of, **34, 50, 54, 82**
  founding of, **34,** 35, 46–47
  grand opening of, **46,** 47, **48,** 49
  interior photographs of, **16–17, 38–39, 44–45, 46, 48**
  MAP meeting at, **76–77**
  meat scale of, **56**
  naming of, 46–47
  during power outages, 83, 86
  reader board of, **50**
  red aprons of, in the 1950s, **61**
  renovation of, 81, **82,** 83
  spirit of, 127
Town & Country Markets, Inc.
  board of, **110**
  community service and, 50, 60–61, 67, 121
  customer service and, 32, 54, 60, 61, 101, 115
  employees of, 32, 60, 126
  expansion of, 57, 59, 70–73, 78, 86, 88, 92–94, 115
  fish and, 38, 87
  flowers and, 31, 66–67
  incorporation of, 47
  information systems department of, **90–91**
  logo of, 72, 101
  mission of, 100–101, 109–11
  name change of, to plural, 110
  organic produce and, 82–83, 86, 87
  vendors and, **87**
Town & Country Poulsbo Market, 111, 117, **118,** 119. *See also* Poulsbo Market Place
Turkey Punch Card, **67**
Tuson, Debbie, 96

U
Umami, 100, 101
University Books, 115
University of Washington, 27, 28, 50

V
Vadalion family, 35
Van Slyke, Michele, 81
Vashon Island, Washington, 14, 15
Viking Mark-It, 59, **60,** 64, 67, 71, 86
Village Foods, 57, 67, 70, 79

W
Washington State Food Dealers Association, 79
Weaver, Scott, **91**
West, Duncan, 116
Weymer, Bill, 71–74, 78, 86
White, Dennis and Bonnie, 82
Williams, Steve, 73, 74, 110, 114
Wilson, Geoff, 50
Wilson, Victoria, **98–99**
Winslow, Washington, 14
Winslow Dock Grocery, 13, 24, **25,** 27
Winslow High School, 20
Winter, David, **44**
Wood, John, 100, 111
Woodward, Milly, 37
Woodward, Walt, 37, 41, 49

Y
Yama, Washington, **18,** 19
Yanick, Miles, 82, 93, 94

ABOUT THE AUTHOR

Russ Banham is the author of fifteen books, including *The Ford Century*, an award-winning history of Ford Motor Company, translated into thirteen languages; *Rocky Mountain Legend*, the best-selling biography of the Coors brewing dynasty; and *Wanderlust*, his new book about journeying in an iconic Airstream travel trailer. The veteran business journalist also has written more than three thousand articles, published by *Forbes*, *The Economist*, *Wall Street Journal*, *CFO*, *Financial Times*, *Euromoney*, *Time*, *U.S. News & World Report*, *Venture*, and *Inc.*, among many others. He lives and works in Edmonds, Washington.